"From the mom̶̶̶̶̶̶̶̶̶̶̶̶̶ fear was coming t̶r̶u̶e̶,̶ ̶I̶ ̶w̶o̶n̶d̶e̶r̶e̶d̶ ̶h̶o̶w̶ ̶h̶e̶r̶ ̶l̶i̶f̶e̶ ̶w̶o̶u̶l̶d̶ ̶c̶h̶a̶n̶g̶e̶.̶ Maria lived through her fear with a relatable humanity while releasing control, uncovering a life of true peace, and writing it all down along the way in this fear-to-freedom handbook. Grab a fresh set of highlighters—you're going to need them."

Myquillyn Smith, author of *The Nesting Place*

"When fear rises up, our first instinct may be to either completely avoid it or fall victim to worst-case scenarios. Maria Furlough offers an alternative, issuing the invitation to break the fear cycle altogether in this gentle and deeply personal book."

Emily P. Freeman, author of *Simply Tuesday*

"Fear finds its paralyzing power in its ability to mentally transport us into imaginary places of pain where the reality of God's presence, power, and provision never show up. Maria Furlough has written a helpful book filled with practical and real-life wisdom for breaking the cycle of fear and faithfully overcoming the harsher realities of life in a painful and broken world."

Larry Osborne, pastor, North Coast Church, and author

"If you've ever had fear that kept you from freedom (and who among us hasn't?), then you have a friend in Maria Furlough. Drawing deeply from her own experience and with vulnerability and courage, Maria encourages us to step forward confidently in Christ. Her story will inspire you; her biblical knowledge and practical wisdom will help you break the fear cycle and move forward into peace. I couldn't put this book down, and I look forward to sharing it with everyone I know who struggles with fear and needs hope for a better future!"

Nicole Unice, pastor, counselor,
and author of *Brave Enough*

"I met Maria Furlough in the middle of my fear. I was speaking at an event near her home. She knew I was battling anxiety so she came to me and prayed the words of Jesus over me: 'Fear not.' That's the woman who is guiding you through this journey. She's someone who shows up to whisper 'fear not' in your ear so you can be the woman God created you to be. In this book, Maria offers welcome wisdom—earned in the trenches—that will help you break the fear cycle and find the peace your heart longs for."

Jennifer Dukes Lee, author of
The Happiness Dare and *Love Idol*

"Maria is a trustworthy spiritual guide to so many people in our church, where she worships and serves. If fear and anxiety are unwelcome parts of your life, don't *read* this book. Instead, *open your life up* to Maria's insightful mentorship by prayerfully interacting with these pages. Her story is both heart-wrenching and heart-freeing. With remarkable insight, she invites us to join her in the peaceful way of life Jesus offers to all."

Dr. Mike Moses, lead pastor, Lake Forest Church, Charlotte, NC; president, Evangelical Presbyterian denomination, 2015; adjunct faculty, Gordon-Conwell Theological Seminary

"When we're afraid, we don't need an optimist to deny our worries or a disciplinarian to condemn our anxiety; we need a truth-telling friend who points us to our Savior. Maria Furlough is that friend. In *Breaking Free from Fear*, she acknowledges our greatest fears and lovingly guides us through God's Word to find our peace and confidence in the Lord."

Marissa Henley, author of *Loving Your Friend Through Cancer*

Breaking Free from Fear

Breaking Free from Fear

How to Find Peace for Your Anxious Heart

Maria Furlough

SPIRE

© 2018 by Maria Furlough

Published by Revell
a division of Baker Publishing Group
PO Box 6287, Grand Rapids, MI 49516-6287
www.revellbooks.com

Spire edition published 2021
ISBN 978-0-8007-4009-2
eISBN 978-1-4934-3137-3

Previously published in 2018 under the title *Breaking the Fear Cycle*

Printed in the United States of America

21   22   23   24   25   26   27   7   6   5   4   3   2   1

To

My *Jesus*

My *Dave*

My sweet, sweet
*Faith, David,
Aaron, Gideon,*
and *Sammy*

Contents

1

Your *Greatest* Fear

What is your *greatest* fear?

You know the one—the one that keeps you up at night, wide awake, unable to fall asleep because anxious thoughts of it coming true swirl around in your brain.

What is your *deepest* fear?

You know the kind—the kind of fear that pops into your mind and then never leaves. The kind of fear that starts with a small, itty-bitty idea and then grows into a full-blown panic attack because you actually have begun to believe that the fear *is* going to come true.

Let's be completely honest. If you are anything like me, you don't even want to take the chance of naming your fear out loud. Why? Well, because there is a tiny voice inside of you that tells you if you say it out loud, you just might jinx yourself. God fearing, God trusting, and God believing though you are, you will not take any chances when it comes to your greatest fear. Your greatest fear is your holy grail. It's yours to keep and obsess over, and you feel like there is simply nothing you can do about it.

Your fear just is. It's part of you, and you have come to accept it. Live with it. Cope with it.

I lived there once too. I lived so entrenched in fear that it became a driving force in my life without me even realizing it. Fear seeped into my relationships, my parenting, my marriage, and my home, and it found such a comfortable place in my days that I stopped fighting it.

This was me: I was the new mom, driving across town to get a much-needed nap at Grandma and Grandpa's house. It was a joyous time. With a healthy baby girl in tow, I drove and thanked God for the gift of her life. I was a mom! A real mom! And it felt like heaven on earth. Then *it* happened. My internal dialogue went something like this:

God! Thank you so much for my daughter, Faith. I love her so much, more than I thought I could love!
   Wait.
   I love her so much.
   I love her too much.
   What would I ever do if I lost her?
   Wait. What would I do if I got in a car accident?
   Wait. I'm driving over a bridge. What would happen if I got into a car accident and flew off this bridge into that body of water? How would I save her? What would I do?
   I can't lose her. I love her too much! I would need to save her.

Then I would go home and do what any reasonable Christ-following woman would do. I would get on Biblegateway.com and search for "verse that promises I will never drive off a bridge with my baby in the back seat."

Ah, thank goodness, there it is! "Nothing bad will ever happen to you, your sweet baby, or any future children or loved ones. I pinkie promise. Thus sayeth the Lord." That's straight from the book of *Keep Dreaming, Maria*.

It's not there! God's Word is *good*. It is holy, reliable, powerful, mysterious, and righteous, and there are no promises that tell me my worst fears will not come true. None, nada, zip! God does not promise us a pain-free existence.

How, then, can I convince my brain *not* to fear the utter destruction of everyone and everything I hold near and dear? Since the Bible doesn't ensure me that these things will *not* happen, and I could not find the Bible verse I was looking for, I went to my second best resource: Google.

Dear Google, what do I do if I drive off a bridge with my one-month-old baby in the back seat? Sincerely yours, Maria.

First, Google says to stay calm (awesome). Then Google says to immediately roll down the windows because that will be your escape route, and soon the water will short-circuit the electricity in most makes and models. Then, while the car is filling up with water, remove your baby from the car seat. After the car is fully submerged, escape through the window with your baby and swim to safety.

There. That feels a little better. Another Band-Aid of control placed over my fear to make me feel a little less anxious. Another case of trying to logically, statistically, and informationally appease my fear instead of diving straight into the heart of the matter.

My fears kept coming. They would come in multiple forms, and my anxious brain would come up with creative ways for my worst fears to come true. Besides driving off bridges, fears would come in the form of

tsunamis (no, I don't live on the coast, but apparently that doesn't matter)

cancer

brain-eating bacteria

choking

poisoning

kidnapping

regular, non-driving-off-bridges car accidents

terrorist attack

loss of a baby

nuclear destruction

I went on, half tackling every obsessive fear that popped into my mind. Then it happened.

I was going on with my everyday life, and the moment we all dread the most *happened*. I learned that one of my worst fears was going to come true. I was pregnant with my fourth child, and at my eighteen-week ultrasound I learned that my sweet baby boy had a fatal condition. He would survive the entire pregnancy, but after he was born he would not live past a few hours.

What do you do then? What do you do when one of your greatest fears actually comes true? All those sleepless nights, endless tears, and racing hearts seemed suddenly justified because I was right! My fears were confirmed! How could I survive this? What do you do when you cannot ignore your fearful heart any longer? When the reality of all of your anxious living slams you in the face? *What can you possibly do?*

May you read this, may you hear me, and may you be reassured that the ending of the story is a good one. It's a glorious one! One in which God is fully victorious over fear *even in* the midst of the worst!

I learned that God has answers for us—good answers, reliable answers—and that there is a way to live in peaceful freedom from our fears. It is not an easy journey, but it is a journey in which God draws nearer than he has ever been before. When we turn to him, when we are in the midst of our fears and we still choose to stay put at the foot of the cross until God lifts us up, then we will find the everlasting peace and hope that our souls so desperately desire.

Let us tackle this question together and head-on: If God's Word does *not* promise us that our worst fears will not come true, then *how* are we supposed to not fear?

John 14:27 states clearly and boldly, "Peace I leave with you; my peace I give you. I do not give to you as the world gives. Do not let your hearts be troubled and do not be afraid."

It's a happy ending. I promise.

It Happened

God knew I was deathly afraid of losing a child. He also knew I was just as afraid of losing a baby during pregnancy. It is a path I knew my own mother had walked, and I politely shared with God that it was not one I ever wanted to go on. I had hopes that God would work on *my* terms because clearly God has given me a rational brain, and my rational brain deducted very logically that losing a baby was not best for my life.

I was eighteen weeks pregnant and so very excited to find out the gender of my fourth child. Naïve and unsuspecting, my husband and I went to the doctor for the ultrasound. On our way into the appointment, I remember casually discussing baby names. If it was a baby girl (which I was positive it would be), we would name her Elizabeth Maria; a baby boy, Gideon Matthew. Surely it was about to be the best day ever. Who doesn't love dreaming about what their little baby will be like?

The ultrasound technician kept asking me questions. I answered them quickly and kept asking her, "Can you tell what it is yet?" I wasn't paying attention to the concerned look on her face. I wasn't even considering the possibility that something might be wrong.

Finally, she announced it! A little boy. The Furlough family was about to add yet another boy to the pack—my fourth child, my third son—Gideon Matthew. Then her voice broke into the silence, "Ma'am, the doctor is going to need to see you. There are some things we did not see well."

No kidneys. No bladder.
My boy had neither.
Without kidneys, there is no amniotic fluid.
Without amniotic fluid, lungs cannot develop.
Without lungs, there is no life. No life.

Hadn't God heard me? Didn't he know that this was not on the list of things I could survive? Whatever happened to "God will not give you more than you can handle"? What happened to that promise? In the doctor's office, I mustered up the courage to ask a question.

"Doctor, will he be stillborn? Will he come soon?"

"No, Maria, your baby boy will live through your entire pregnancy. He will go full term, and then he will live only for minutes or hours. I'm so sorry, Maria."

Through my sobbing, I never felt mad at God. I never questioned his goodness or blamed him. But the fear that had gripped me for so long turned into terror, and I literally felt like I was going to die from the burden of sadness, pain, and anxiety.

I feared being pregnant with a child who was not going to live.

I feared people making comments in public about my pregnant belly.

I feared my three older children living in sadness, fear, and confusion.

I feared labor.

I feared holding him and watching him die.

I feared my milk coming in with no baby to feed.

I feared pregnancy weight gain, with no baby to show for it.

I feared loving him too much.

I feared death.

I feared pain.

This time was different. My fears were based on actual circumstances! No longer hearsay or made-up scenarios, this was real and this was happening. The Band-Aids I had created for myself no longer worked.

I no longer had a choice; I *had* to fight fear head-on. I had to go right to the heart of my fear, sword in hand, and kill fear dead once and for all. If I didn't kill the fear, the fear was going to kill me.

Day in and day out, from November 22, the day of Gideon's diagnosis, until March 31, the day when Gideon was born, I fought my fear. With God by my side, his Word my only hope, and through the miraculous help of the Holy Spirit, God taught me how to take aim at my fears.

My prayer for you is this: may you experience the freedom I experienced without ever having to live through the pain. *My* fear? It was redeemed through the life and death of my baby boy Gideon. With God at my side, I fought fear and I fought it *hard*, and God taught me a battle plan that works. May it work for you too. May it bring you hope and freedom, and may you embark with confidence on this journey, knowing full well that if he can heal a fearful soul like mine, he can heal yours too.

> If I didn't kill the fear, the fear was going to kill me.

My assurance to you begins with this: Jesus is not a liar. If Jesus knew that the command "do not be afraid" was unattainable, he would not have asked us to do this.

In John 14, Jesus himself is at the precipice of torture. The night before he died, hours before he was about to sweat blood from anguish, he confidently spoke these words to his disciples: "*Peace* I leave with you; my peace I give you. I do not give to you as the world gives. *Do not* let your hearts be troubled and *do not* be afraid" (v. 27, emphasis added). Let the words of our Savior sink in for a second, and reflect on the fact that he does not lead us astray.

Peace he leaves. What does that mean? Earlier in John 14, Jesus said, "All this I have spoken while still with you. But the Advocate [the Counselor], the Holy Spirit, whom the Father will send in my name, will teach you all things and will remind you of everything I have said to you" (vv. 25–26). Peace he leaves with us; his Holy Spirit he gives to us. Jesus does not give to us as the world gives to us! His gift of peace cannot be quantified; it cannot be counted or measured.

It cannot be seen nor touched, but it *is* real. No, not as the world gives. Not the world that constantly reminds us that we have *much* to fear. Not the world that teaches us that we are not good enough, we don't make enough, we are not worth enough, and we can't control enough. We cannot look to Jesus to solve our fears with percentages, facts, and reassurances. But we can look to him to solve them *well*.

Do not let your hearts be troubled.

My friend, our hearts *are* troubled, aren't they? But take it from Jesus. Take it from a man (*fully* man) who spoke these very words before he was about to surrender his life for us. Our hearts do not have to *stay* troubled.

Do not be afraid. *Do not be afraid.*

Could it be? Could it really be true? Can we really not be afraid? I say it *can* be true. I say through God's help we can surely make it true in our lives. Jesus loves us, does not lie to us, and would not call us to something we cannot achieve.

We have given in to the lie that our fearful and anxious thoughts are more powerful than we are. We have bought into the falsity that what the world has to give is more reliable and trustworthy than what God has to give. Our thoughts do not need to rule us. We have a Savior, a holy Counselor, and a good Father who wants to do the job of being our most reliable and trustworthy source.

Today, may we take the stand to journey together. May we figure out how to fight fear and walk the road toward peace hand in hand.

Your Journey

Your journey starts here. Grab a journal, a pen, and a Bible and find a quiet place—whatever you need to make this *your time*. Your time to process and pour out and let God into the places you have been afraid to let him into. This might not be pretty, it might get hard, but will you try? Will you come with me on this journey? Will you bring into your days, your moments, and your life opportunities to let God speak into your fears? Will you allow yourself the space and the quiet to listen?

Many times I think that fears speak loudest in the silence. I think we are afraid to sit and listen because we fear what we are going to hear. Our brains can be so cruel sometimes. When we sit in the quiet, all the what-ifs tend to come. Let it happen. This time, just this once, in that moment when you begin your time of journaling and reflection, let all the fears pile up. Let them out. Make a list. Make it descriptive. Make it truthful and clear and vulnerable. You can rip it up later if you need to, but for now, make the fears real. God works in the light and not in the darkness. The only one suffering from your deepest, darkest fears is you. Bring them out! Let them flow. Give them over to a God who is willing to receive them. Will you be brave with me? I know you can do it. I know you can because you were brave enough to pick up this book and make it to this point. You have courage in you. Believe in it, tap into it, and go.

Following are some questions to work through. May I pray for you before you begin?

Father, we are about to go to a place with you that is deep and dark and painful. It hurts, and if we have to go there, we only want to go there with you! Father, will you come now? Will you walk on this journey with us? Will you whisper to us in the quiet? When the fears pour out onto the pages, I pray, God, that there you will be. I pray that your Holy Spirit will infiltrate our hearts and that there will be no denying you are here and you are good. I pray that we will not shy away from the painful or the difficult. Instead, I pray that we will invite you in. That we will lean into you with our pain and our fears. I pray that we will be brave enough now to dig into the places to which we are afraid to journey. I pray, God, that as we sit with you, you will be our comforter, our strength, and our guide. Father, with expectancy and in the powerful name of Jesus, I pray. Amen.

Questions for Reflection

1. What are the things in life that you are most afraid of?
2. Where are the places you most fear your thoughts going to?
3. What are your fears? Call them out by name.
4. Can you trust God with your fears? When you look at your tear-drenched list, can you see God between the lines?

5. Does your faith in God tell you that he can handle them all, that he is big enough, strong enough, and loving enough? Or does your list tell you that God is too small, too weak, and uncaring?

2

You Do Have
a Choice

Jesus spoke the words of John 14:27 on the eve of great pain and change. Jesus's charge to "not be afraid" did not come during a time when he had nothing to fear. In fact, he said this on the night before his own death on the cross. His disciples were soon to watch their friend and teacher die. They were about to be persecuted themselves, and many of them would lose their own lives at a young age in the name of Jesus. How could he say this, then? Could it be that fearlessness is not based on circumstance? What, then, is it based on?

I can picture Jesus sitting across from his loved ones, a sense of urgency in his voice as he shared his last teachings before his death. He needed them to pay attention. Jesus knew they would need something to fall back on when times got hard. He knew that in the middle of fearful circumstances and unknown outcomes his disciples would need something strong to lean on.

Jesus also knew that fearful times were coming for them. He knew they were going to be hunted, persecuted, and tortured, and he knew they were going to be tempted to be afraid. Rightly so. We can jive with that equation. We can understand being fearful in scary circumstances because it comes naturally to us; we are human. We are made for so much more than this world, but while we are in it, we are going to feel uncomfortable, out of control, and afraid of what *could* happen. But Jesus does not give to us as the world gives, and so our reaction to fear must not be of this world either.

> You cannot stop fear from coming, but it is your choice whether you are going to *let it in*.

Jesus told his disciples not to *let* their hearts be troubled. Do not *let* them. But how can this be, Jesus? I don't "let" my heart fear, I don't "let" my mind worry, I don't "let" my spirit doubt. They just do!

May you allow God to whisper to you the sweet words he whispered to me as I studied these verses: "No, child, you cannot stop fear from coming, but it is your choice whether you are going to *let it in*." A choice? It's never felt like a choice, so how is that at all possible?

Please don't miss this. Fear will come. It is a part of being human (*not* of God) that our bodies fear the unknown, the painful, and the scary things of this world. Yes, fear will absolutely come. But it is our choice how much dominion we are going to allow fear to have over our lives. It is our choice whether we will rule over our fear or we will let our fear rule over us.

Are You a Saul or a David?

If God charges us not to be afraid, what are we to do when fears come? Joshua 1:9 tells us, "Have I not commanded you? Be strong and courageous. Do not be afraid; do not be discouraged, for the LORD your God will be with you wherever you go."

God frequently tells his children in the Bible not to be afraid. To instead be strong and courageous, for the Lord your God will be with you. But what does this actually look like? What does this mean for our everyday lives and the choices we face? I believe God gives us examples, glimpses that reveal that, yes, it is possible to be strong and courageous in the face of our fears. He uses his Word and his people to show us what it looks like when his commands are lived out and believed in. He does this to encourage and remind us that we are not alone, that we are never alone.

Many of us have heard the biblical stories of Saul and David. Saul was chosen by the people of Israel to be their first king, and then God chose his successor, David. Saul and David had a tumultuous relationship, to say the least, and as David's time to reign was approaching, Saul became crippled by fear. It is interesting to read their stories through the lens of how each of them handled their fearful thoughts.

Read with me first a few verses about Saul.

Then Saul said to Samuel, "I have sinned. I violated the LORD's command and your instructions. I was afraid of the men and so I gave in to them." (1 Sam. 15:24)

Saul was afraid of David, because the LORD was with David but had departed from Saul. So he sent David away from him and gave him command over a thousand men, and David led the troops in their campaigns. In everything he did he had great success, because the LORD was with him. When Saul saw how successful he was, he was afraid of him. But all Israel and Judah loved David, because he led them in their campaigns. (1 Sam. 18:12–16)

In verse 24, Saul is explaining to Samuel why he chose to disobey the Lord. You see, God asked him to do one thing, and he chose to do another. Why? Because he was afraid of his men. He had before him two options: do what God wanted him to do or do what his men wanted him to do. In his fear, he chose to disobey God. This very choice was the beginning of the end of his kingship over Israel.

Because of his fear-based choice, Saul disobeyed the Lord, and God decided it was time for a new king. He chose David, and verse 14 tells us that "the LORD was with him." Saul once more became afraid: afraid of David's power, afraid of David's popularity, and afraid of David's closeness with the Lord. Fears kept coming for Saul, so much so that he chased after David and spent his last days trying to get revenge on the man he feared. Saul was fearful and chose to *react to his fear*. These fear-based reactions were the demise of Saul. He stopped listening to God, and he stopped listening to reason. He allowed fear to rule him until the very end.

We can do the same thing.

I know I did.

I never realized how reactive I had become to my fears until I received Gideon's diagnosis. It hit me painfully when I was offered the option to end my pregnancy with Gideon early. The doctors told us it was "our choice" and that they would support us in whatever we decided. They said most families who receive a fatal diagnosis like Gideon's choose to end the pregnancy early since there is nothing that can be done to save the baby.

At the time, this made complete sense to me. My fears had utterly and completely crippled me. I saw no solution other than to try to "skip" the more long-lasting pain. I felt I needed to wriggle out from underneath my painful circumstance as soon as possible and to run away from the fears. I did not see that I was *choosing* to make decisions based on my fears. I gave full power to fear and made my decisions accordingly.

I was afraid to watch Gideon die. My solution: bring him into the world at eighteen weeks so he would pass away peacefully during labor.

I was afraid to watch my older children suffer. My solution: have Gideon at eighteen weeks alone in the hospital and tell the children he simply went to heaven early.

I was afraid to fall more in love with Gideon and thus make his dying even harder. My solution: deliver him early so I would have fewer days to fall in love with him.

31

I was afraid of being in public visibly pregnant and having people say, "Congratulations!" My solution: end the pregnancy before my belly began to show.

Friends, I want to confess to you, I made the choice to go to the hospital on December 2 to bring Gideon into the world early. I let fear rule over me, and I sit here and shudder at the thought of all that would have been lost in my life, in my family members' lives, and in Gideon's life if God had allowed my own fearful decision to reign.

There has got to be a better way to deal with fear when it comes. There has got to be a better answer, a better plan, a healthier, faith-filled way to react to the many and understandable fearful thoughts that come our way. I believe David gives us some examples of a better way.

Saul wanted and needed to kill David in order to feel secure and unafraid again. So David had to run. It was his only chance for survival. While he was running, he wrote some psalms, his praises and prayers to God. Let's take a look at a couple and see what David did when he was afraid.

> Listen to my prayer, O God,
> > do not ignore my plea;
> > hear me and answer me.
> My thoughts trouble me and I am distraught
> > because of what my enemy is saying,
> > because of the threats of the wicked;
> for they bring down suffering on me
> > and assail me in their anger.

My heart is in anguish within me;
    the terrors of death have fallen on me.
Fear and trembling have beset me;
    horror has overwhelmed me.
I said, "Oh, that I had the wings of a dove!
    I would fly away and be at rest.
I would flee far away
    and stay in the desert;
I would hurry to my place of shelter,
    far from the tempest and storm."

Lord, confuse the wicked, confound their words,
    for I see violence and strife in the city.
Day and night they prowl about on its walls;
    malice and abuse are within it.
Destructive forces are at work in the city;
    threats and lies never leave its streets.

If an enemy were insulting me,
    I could endure it;
if a foe were rising against me,
    I could hide.
But it is you, a man like myself,
    my companion, my close friend,
with whom I once enjoyed sweet fellowship
    at the house of God,
as we walked about
    among the worshipers.

Let death take my enemies by surprise;
    let them go down alive to the realm of the dead,
    for evil finds lodging among them.

As for me, I call to God,
    and the LORD saves me.
Evening, morning and noon
    I cry out in distress,
    and he hears my voice.
He rescues me unharmed
    from the battle waged against me,
    even though many oppose me.
God, who is enthroned from of old,
    who does not change—
he will hear them and humble them,
    because they have no fear of God.

My companion attacks his friends;
    he violates his covenant.
His talk is smooth as butter,
    yet war is in his heart;
his words are more soothing than oil,
    yet they are drawn swords.

Cast your cares on the LORD
    and he will sustain you;
he will never let
    the righteous be shaken.
But you, God, will bring down the wicked
    into the pit of decay;
the bloodthirsty and deceitful
    will not live out half their days.

But as for me, I trust in you. (Ps. 55)

When I am afraid, I put my trust in you.
    In God, whose word I praise—

in God I trust and am not afraid.
What can mere mortals do to me? (Ps. 56:3–4)

David's fears were intense, and they were many. But in his fear he went straight to the throne of God, to the One who loved him and cared for him. He cried out in honesty and boldness and did not hold back! I believe we can learn a lot from David. In these two psalms, we might even find a battle plan to wage war against fear when it comes. Before reacting to it, before falling under its control, you can instead first do what David did.

He asked God to listen to him. Get God's attention! There is passion in David's voice. We do not always need to pray in a quiet whisper. Sometimes a desperate yell is just what the doctor ordered.

He told God he was afraid. Pour out to him how afraid you are. Tell God you are at the very bottom; fear surrounds you, and you don't know what to do. Give all of it over to a loving Father who is waiting to hear.

He unpacked his crazy thoughts. David literally asked God to strike Saul and all his men dead. I'm pretty sure this proves that we cannot say anything that surprises God. Don't sugar-coat the truth or your feelings. Don't allow shame or guilt to hinder your prayers. Pour it all out, in full detail.

He claimed trust in God. Choose to surrender your fear to God and claim instead to trust: *when* I am afraid, I will trust in you, Lord. There is power in our prayers, in our words. When you run out of your own words, use the ones God provides in Scripture. In seasons when fear comes barreling in on a daily basis, put Psalm 56:3–4 up where you can see it. Read these verses out loud, and stake claim to the power they hold.

He acknowledged God's promises. "Cast your cares on the LORD and he will sustain you" (Ps. 55:22). God promises to sustain you. He promises; this means he *will.*

He left his fear with God. Tomorrow the fear may return, but today, leave it with God.

When I was in the middle of my fear-filled choice, preparing for Gideon to come early, all I had in me was one faith-filled, David-like prayer. I softly uttered it as I went to bed the night before I was to go to the hospital: *Father, I am afraid, but may your will be done.* You see, God is good and merciful, and we do not need a huge dose of faith to bring our fear to him. We need only a little tiny bit. As my head hit the pillow that night, God began to meet me in my fear. Yes, I went to the hospital to have Gideon early. But as I lay on the hospital bed that morning, a little bit of courage began to rise up inside of me. While the doctor started to administer the induction medicine, I prayed this prayer:

> *God, this does not feel right to me. I don't feel like I should be here, but, Lord, I am so afraid! I cannot see past my fear and my hurt, and so, Lord, my only choice now is to look to you. The circumstances around me are so far out of my control. Here I am! I am checked into a hospital, the doctors are giving me medicine to bring Gideon into the world today, my baby has a fatal condition, and, Father, I am scared because this is all my eyes can see. Instead,*

*God, right here in this hospital room, I pray that you will
bring my eyes to you! I also pray, God, that you will save
me from this bed. Get me out of this place, Lord. Forgive
me for my fearful decision. I trusted in my fear rather than
you, and I am sorry. Save me, Lord. Save my baby. Amen.*

The induction medicine never really took. Seven hours in,
I asked the doctor what was taking so long. I was informed
that inductions that take place early in pregnancy can take up
to four days. In four days I was supposed to take my daughter to New York City for the first time. I couldn't bear the
thought of telling her we couldn't go, and so I asked the question that changed my life forever: "Will I be able to make it
to my trip?"

"Well," they said, "you can just go home and come back
here Tuesday if you want." Or I can go home and come back
never if I want!

A second chance. God gave me a second chance! I left
that hospital mad at my fear. How had I let it run so deep as
to almost allow it to take from me one of the greatest days I
would ever experience? Four months later on March 31, I experienced the single most powerful day of my life. Fear nearly
took that from me. No more. Not for me, and not for you.

When we make the choice to trust God, we become able
to do amazing things. Twice David had the opportunity to
easily kill Saul outright, and both times David chose to spare
him. Even after David prayed for God to kill Saul for him!
Why? Because David didn't need Saul to die to kill his fear;
he just had to trust God with it.

As for me, I wish I could say that what came next was easy. That all it took was one miraculously answered prayer, and all my fears ran to the wayside. That wasn't the case. Fears continued to assault me, and I embarked on a four-month daily battle with worry and terrifying thoughts. But what happened is that, day by day, God revealed to me his battle plan over fear. He pulled back the curtain just a little and let me peek into the heavenly power of his reigning peace. I believe he will do that for you too.

Your Journey

Fear can make us do crazy things. Sometimes, without us even realizing it, we put fear in the driver's seat of our lives. Today, as you take time in your quiet place with pen, journal, and Bible in hand, I pray that you might begin to look at some examples in your own life—times and situations when you acted out of fear. Maybe some were so gripping that you took the nearest exit door just to get away from the pain.

This is not meant to be a time of regret but one of learning. And not only learning from past experiences but also learning *about* you. Take an inventory of your heart, actions, and fears. But first, take some time in the quiet and pour your heart out, in ink, to the Lord.

Father, today we come to you, and we ask you to teach us. Where are the places in our lives that we have been blind to fear? Will you gently reveal to us the times in our lives when we have let fear be in the driver's seat? God, will you work sweetly and kindly with us? Our hearts are open to your working, yet they are tender still. We desire to grow, and I pray that you will speak now in ways that are encouraging to our spirits and affirming of your promises. It is because we love you and we trust you that we come to you now. In the powerful name of Jesus, I pray. Amen.

Questions for Reflection

1. What happens in your brain, in your thinking, when anxious thoughts come to you?
2. Do you stew in them over and over again, diving deep into every fear-drenched detail?
3. What are some times in your life when you made decisions based on your fears?
4. What were the results of those decisions?
5. Second Corinthians 10:5 says, "We demolish arguments and every pretension that sets itself up against the knowledge of God, and we take captive every thought to make it obedient to Christ." What are some ways, notes, and prayers you can use to help take those fearful thoughts captive?
6. Will you practice taking those thoughts captive? Practice making the choice to let the fear-filled thoughts go instead of holding on to them and making decisions based on them.

3

Fear and
Future Telling

It's 11:36 p.m. I look at the clock and say to myself, *Where is he? He said he would be back by 10:00. I should call him.*

Ring, ring, ring. A thousand times, *ring*. No answer, of course. *Well, he never picks up his phone anyway.*

11:42 p.m. Maybe I'll send him a text. I say, "Hey, honey, it's after 11:30. Just checking in to make sure you're okay."

11:50 p.m. *Where the heck is he? I'm calling again.*

Ring. Still no answer.

11:55 p.m. Call again. No answer.

Now, here comes the fun part. The part I am wondering if you can at all relate to. Let's try this mental rundown on for size to see if it fits.

He's dead! That's it! I know he is dead! He got into a car crash on his way home at 10:30, and the paramedics rushed him to the hospital, and now the local police are just mustering up enough courage to come knock on my door to let me know that my husband has passed away. Then I will melt on the floor in a blubbering mess, my children will be subjected to a life of missing their father, we will never be the same, and I will want to die from sorrow and grief. Then I will turn into the world's most terribly pathetic mother, and my children will end up hating me. This night is clearly the beginning of the end!

Insert husband walking through the door. "Hey, hon."

"Hey, hon? Hey, hon?! Are you kidding me? You couldn't just call to let me know you were going to run late?"

"Jeesh, lay off me. Stop worrying so much."

Grrr. Oh to be a person who does not struggle with fear. But, alas, this is me, and I am wondering if it is you too.

In case you haven't noticed, there is something that all my fearful thoughts have in common. Whether it is fearing my husband dying in a car crash, fearing my kids getting a bad health diagnosis, or fearing the possibility of losing a job, any and all fears take my mind out of the present and into the future. These anxious thoughts distract me from what I am experiencing in the *now* and cause me to imagine a series of events that *could* happen later.

The same thing happened during my pregnancy with Gideon. I took all the things that people told me *could* happen when Gideon came, and my fear warped them into a litany of worst-case scenarios. My brain would swirl and my heart rate would rise, and I would find myself consumed with the many terrible things that my mind decided were about to unfold. I began to take note of a pattern.

First, all my fears took place in the future. None of them included *today's reality*. For example, if I was headed to a doctor's appointment or one of my children asked me a difficult question about death, feelings of nervousness might arise. But I would take a deep breath, say a prayer, and tackle the scenario in my path. Fear was much different. Fear would take a small nugget of a what-if, and my thoughts would explode it into a full-blown disaster. Fearful thinking took me out of today's actual happenings and into an attempt to predict tomorrow.

Second, God was never there. In all of my fearful fabrications, never once did I insert the presence and the power of the living God. My brain would fixate only on the tangible and the horrific facts, not taking into consideration that God shows up in supernatural ways in times of suffering, tragedy, and trials. My fearful thoughts never bothered to include God.

Third, once the fearful thoughts started, it was tough to make them stop. As soon as I allowed my brain to elaborate on my fantasy, it became very hard for me to turn the ship around. Take the fear of a car accident. The old Maria would have called my husband fifty-one times. I would sit there and attempt to get control of myself, but once my fear got past a certain point, it became very difficult to get back to reality. This was especially true for me in the weeks after we decided to carry Gideon to full term. In those early days, my heart was still very much struggling to accept the reality of the coming months. A thought would pop into my mind: *What is it going to be like to watch Gideon die? It is going to be terribly awful; it is going to be virtually impossible. He is going to suffer, I won't be able to save him, that vision will stay with me, and I will be tortured by that imagery forever. I can't do this. I can't do this.* One time I even called a different part of the state to see if I could travel there and have Gideon at twenty-four weeks instead of waiting the full forty weeks. My freight train of fear was barreling down the tracks at breakneck speed, and I literally needed a miracle to turn things around.

Future Telling Is God's Job

I'll never forget the first time I read the tragic story of Job in the Bible. It begins with Job losing everything. His children, his possessions, and his health—all wiped out. In one fell swoop, he goes from being "the greatest man among all people of the East" (Job 1:3) to his wife advising him, "Are you still maintaining your integrity? Curse God and die!" (2:9). I remember thinking, *How could you, God? How could you let all that happen?*

Job didn't just imagine what might happen—he lived out every worst fear imaginable. If something is on your list of fears, it probably happened to Job. The book of Job enthralls people who struggle with fear. We wish that one time we could read it and it would suddenly end with, "Nah, just kidding. None of that stuff happened to Job because no bad stuff ever happens to good people!" Honestly, we hope the story will change. But it never does. Job always loses all he owned, always loses all his children, and always becomes sick. His wife always curses God, and his friends always fail him. Every time, same story: an amazing man of God and all his worst fears come true.

The book of Job is forty-two chapters long. The calamities all occur in the first two chapters! So forty more chapters of what? In most of them, Job is time skipping. And rightly so. He wants to know why. He digs back through his past and curses it. He seeks fervently for understanding. If he could just have an answer, if he could skip ahead and know the ending, then he would feel better. And can you blame him? "That's right, you go, Job! You should ask those questions because we want to know the answers too!" Make no mistake, Job never does curse God. He curses the day he was born, but never God. In Job 3, he says:

> May the day of my birth perish,
>   and the night that said, "A boy is conceived!"
> That day—may it turn to darkness;
>   may God above not care about it;
>   may no light shine on it. (vv. 3–4)

But Job wonders—he asks, he seeks, and he speculates. He pleads and begs for all the hows and whys. For over thirty chapters, he cries out in the torment of his reality. He doesn't ever question God's goodness. Job keeps his faith and his integrity. All he wants is a little bit of understanding into his past, his present, and his future. He wants a peek into what God knows.

Finally, in chapter 38, the Lord speaks. My heart pounding through my chest, I gripped my Bible with both hands the first time I read Job. I was *so* excited! I just knew that God was going to say, "Job! I feel terrible that you are going through this, and I don't blame you at all for all your questions. Because you are so faithful to me, I am now going to tell you why I have allowed this to happen to you!"

Here it comes. I couldn't wait any longer! Then I read Job 38:1–7:

> Then the LORD spoke to Job out of the storm. He said:
>
> *"Who is this that obscures my plans*
>   *with words without knowledge?*
> Brace yourself like a man;
>   I will question you,
>   and you shall answer me.
>
> *"Where were you when I laid the earth's foundation?*
>   *Tell me, if you understand.*
> Who marked off its dimensions? Surely you know!
>   Who stretched a measuring line across it?
> On what were its footings set,
>   or who laid its cornerstone—
> while the morning stars sang together
>   and all the angels shouted for joy?" (emphasis
>   added)

Wait. What? Did I read that correctly? God, didn't you get the memo about losing all his children, painful sores from head to toe, not a penny to his name? I think you must have gotten the wrong man! Then, "Who is this that obscures my plans with words without knowledge?" and "Where were you when I laid the earth's foundation?" Lord, is that not harsh? Is that not brutal?

Then it hit me. God was simply taking back what was rightfully his to begin with: his sovereignty. God was reminding Job that he does not see the world with omniscient power—but God does! God is best for the task of unfolding the details of Job's life. Surely, if God can lay the foundations of the earth, he can take care of us too. Surely, if God can place the stars in the sky, he can also take care of our futures. And just as surely, if God can remind Job in his suffering, he can remind us too.

Every time I give in to a fearful thought, I am taking a bite from the fruit of the tree of the knowledge of good and evil all over again. I am deciding, like Adam and Eve, that God's reign over my future is not good enough for me; no, I need to try to tackle it myself. Trouble is, my brain was not created for such a thing. In our finite minds, we cannot comprehend the complexities of our futures. We *can* calculate all the what-ifs and the whys, and so we fear. We fear because ultimately we wonder if we can trust God to do his job well.

> Would you be willing, with me, to give God his job back?

Would you be willing, with me, to give God his job back? Would you be willing to try to take one brave and faithful step toward fearless living by taking captive any and all thoughts that fabricate a future we do not yet know will come true? Will you try?

The Battle Plan

This is no small thing. I know this because I lived it. I woke up every morning and waged war against my fearful future telling. To have any hope of real change, I had to come up with a battle plan.

This is not just one of those "yeah, I'll try to get better at that" type things. No, this is an "I must *have a plan* of what to do when my brain starts getting on the fear train into the future" type thing.

Step 1: Identify a future fear the second it pops into your mind. Ask yourself the following questions: Is this thought about something I know to be true right now, or am I trying to tell the future? Is this fearful thought based on something that *is* true, or is it based on something that I am imagining *could* come true? Call it out. Immediately identify a future-based fear when it comes, and stop it dead in its tracks.

Step 2: Talk to yourself. Sounds funny I know, but try it. State the future-based fear out loud, talk to yourself about it, write it down, do whatever you need to do to get your brain back into the moment. Make yourself take a pause in your thinking. Try deep breaths, prayers, anything!

Step 3: Ask yourself this question: What do I know *to be true right now?* Ask yourself, and then answer it. In the story of the car accident I shared earlier, my answer would sound something like this: what I know to be true right now is that my husband is not home yet, my kids are happily asleep in their beds, I am sitting here watching a show, and I have received no bad news.

Step 4: Focus on blessings. Combat negative with positive. List all the blessings, big and small, you have in your life right at this moment. Focus on them, go through them, smile about them, thank God for them. Try going through the "ABCs of Blessings," naming a blessing in your life for every letter of the alphabet.

Step 5: Name God's truths. There is power in God's Word. It is alive, it is sharp, and it is helpful (Heb. 4:12). Reciting Scripture helps. It isn't one of those things you have to feel or believe. You simply have to *do it.* The power is in the promises, and they simply need to be uttered. So utter them over and over and do not stop until you notice a shift in your peacefulness. Following are some of the verses that helped me. I wrote them on my hand, taped them on my bathroom mirror, posted them on my kitchen cabinets. I put them up everywhere and anywhere so that when I needed them, they were easily accessible.

Therefore do not worry about tomorrow, for tomorrow will worry about itself. Each day has enough trouble of its own. (Matt. 6:34)

Have no fear of sudden disaster
    or of the ruin that overtakes the wicked,
for the LORD will be at your side
    and will keep your foot from being snared.
        (Prov. 3:25–26)

She is clothed with strength and dignity;
    she can laugh at the days to come. (Prov. 31:25)

You will keep in perfect peace
　　those whose minds are steadfast,
　　because they trust in you.
Trust in the LORD forever,
　　for the LORD, the LORD himself, is the Rock
　　　　eternal. (Isa. 26:3–4)

Then Job replied to the LORD:

"I know that you can do all things;
　　no purpose of yours can be thwarted.
You asked, 'Who is this that obscures my plans
　　without knowledge?'
　　Surely I spoke of things I did not understand,
　　things too wonderful for me to know."
　　　　(Job 42:1–3)

Your Journey

When you picture the future, do you see God there? Too often, when our brains are fixed on the worst-case scenario, we don't imagine God meeting us there. Surely *that* (whatever "that" is for you) would be so terrible even God could not reach me in that place. As a result, it's tempting to convince ourselves that clearly *we* know what is best. Our logic and analysis lead us to believe that we, and we alone, know the best, nicest, and loveliest plan for the future. The truth is, we take God right out of the picture.

As you venture into some time alone with God, I ask you to sit with him for a minute. Picture in your mind your days unfolding before you—the good, the bad, the feared, the coveted. What do you see? Are you so convinced that your way is the *only* way? Do you see happiness *if*, and only *if*, God answers your prayers exactly the way you want him to? Give God your plans and ask him if you are holding too tightly to the future you have envisioned for yourself. Search your heart to discover whether you have made future planning your job instead of God's job.

> *Father, as we come to sit with you now, we confess that our brains are whirling a thousand miles an hour. You have given us the gifts of intellect, planning, and strategizing, yet they are gifts we want to submit to you first. We confess that only our plans seem like good ones. We confess that many times we feel that if things don't go as we plan, we will be broken beyond compare. I pray that when we think of the future, we will think of you first. Reveal to us, Lord, what your Word says about our coming days. Show us the strength we need to live one moment at a time, simply being faithful with each footstep. As we come to you now, I pray that you will speak. I pray that you will give us the courage to be honest with you. I pray that we will become more like Job as we confess with our lips, "Forgive us, Lord, for we spoke of things too wonderful for us to understand." You are good. You are trustworthy. We love you. It's in the powerful name of Jesus that I pray. Amen.*

Questions for Reflection

1. Do you fear the future?
2. Do you imagine all the terrible things that could, might, or will go wrong?
3. When you fear the future, do you imagine God being there, or are your thoughts void of the presence of God?
4. Can you trust God and let the future be his territory?
5. Right now, what details about your future can you give to him?
6. Do you believe that God knows better than you do?
7. What is true and beautiful in your life right now?

4

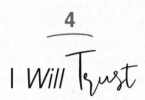

I Will Trust

Certain fears cannot even be spoken.

I get it. There are some fears that run so deep and are so painful that you will not even let your lips utter them out loud. It is because even the mere idea of the fear coming true causes such discomfort that you block it out.

No, some fears cannot even be spoken out loud.

But what if we forced ourselves to go there? What if we muscled past our basic instincts and made our brains entertain the details of our deepest fears? What would happen? Could it possibly hurt more than it already does? Would the thoughts themselves be enough to break our hearts to pieces? Would we survive?

It sounds cruel. At first, it sounds like self-mutilation, self-torture, self-inflicted suffering. So why on earth would I even entertain the idea? Well, I believe that keeping things in the dark, hidden and unaddressed, allows Satan to do his best work. Even though we might not be facing our fears, Satan is aware of them in the dark recesses of our souls and is feeding them.

When I was pregnant with Gideon, I found myself in deep and painful fear every day. Fear when I fell asleep at night, fear when I woke up. Fear when I was merely trying to go through the everyday motions and could hardly move. I was desperate for relief, and so I took drastic measures. In my helplessness toward my fears, I found the courage to do something I had never done before. I removed my hands from my ears, I opened my eyes, I stopped yelling at the fears to go away, and I turned around and looked them straight in the eye.

My worst fears—straight in the eye.

I studied them. I searched deep and wide. I asked the tough questions: Why am I afraid of you? What is it about you that keeps me up at night and trembling with fear? What power do you have over my life?

I named all the yucky, gory details. I allowed the fears to play out, full force, from beginning to end in my mind. I became a student of all my worst and darkest fears.

At the end of every scenario, every single time, the answer was still the same: yes, Lord, even then, I *will* trust in you.

You Can Do This

I know you don't want to face your fears. I know this is absolutely the *worst* idea that anyone has ever come up with since the beginning of time! I know that right now you are tempted to say no. There is *no way* I am entertaining the idea of facing my worst fears.

Six months after losing Gideon, I became pregnant again. You can imagine the litany of fears that enveloped my brain. We are smart people, and it is because we are smart that we are unsuccessful at rationalizing away our fears. I could not tell myself that I definitely would not lose another baby because I did not know that to be true. After all, Gideon's diagnosis was 1/80,000, so I had already beaten the odds once. The Band-Aids of reason, statistics, and percentages no longer tricked my brain out of fearing. Every time I tried to tackle them by avoiding them, the fears only came back stronger.

I had to face them, again.

Me: What if I lose this baby too? What if I have to suffer again the way I did before? What if the heartache breaks me this time? What if I have to watch my children lose another sibling?

God: What if you did?

Me: Wait. What do you mean "What if I did?" That does not make me feel very good!

God: What if you did lose this baby too? What is it you are afraid of?

Me: I am afraid of all the pain and the hurt and the loss and the death. I am afraid of everything I just went through.

God: Yes, sweet girl, what if you had to go through that all over again? Do you believe I would be there for you? Would you trust me to get you through it like I did last time? Did I not prove myself trustworthy?

Me: Yes, Father. The answer is yes. I know that you did not let me down last time, and I know you would not start now. Yes, I trust that you would take care of me.

God: What about your children? Do you trust that I would take care of them too?

Me: Yes, I know you would take care of them too.

The real and the honest-to-goodness truth is that we have no promises to cling to that what we fear the most won't happen. I wish we did; I so wish there was an escape route. There just isn't, and the sooner we allow ourselves to address the truth about our fears, the sooner we can allow God in to redeem them.

If you are like me, you don't really trust that God will be there because you can't actually comprehend what on earth he could do for you. After all, your child would still be sick or dying, your spouse would still have left, your job would still be gone, the house would still be taken, your children would still be running away from you. The actual circumstance of the fear wouldn't change, and so what then could he possibly do for you?

This is where the miracle comes in. This is where faith is defined, and we ask ourselves if we really believe in the things unseen. Do we believe that there is something greater than what our fingers can touch and what our eyes can see?

May we take hope in the survival of those who have gone before us. May we believe their testimony, their story, to be true, and may we take heart in the knowledge that God comes alive in new ways to those in the midst of the worst.

Poor Jeremiah. Every time I read his story in the Bible my heart breaks for him. What a terrible job he had; his sole purpose was to communicate God's warning message to the people of Israel that destruction was coming! People hated the guy. Who can blame them? Jeremiah walked around with messages full of impending doom. Imagine the comments: "Who brought the negative Nancy? Get him out of here." But God's message was clear: his people had turned their backs on him, and as a result, the desolation of Israel was coming. In Jeremiah 20, he says to God, "If I say, 'I will not mention him or speak any more in his name,' his word is in my heart like a fire, a fire shut up in my bones. I am weary of holding it in; indeed, I cannot" (v. 9). Even when Jeremiah tried to be done, he simply could not keep God's message in. It had to be told. But hearts were hard, stubbornness ran rampant, and the Israelites ignored Jeremiah's warning.

Destruction came.

It's tempting to skip over the details of what the destruction of Israel looked like. Cities burning and whole civilizations being taken to the ground are not things we have experienced much in our corner of history. But when you break it down, it looks very much like a worst nightmare coming true.

Jobs lost.

Homes burned.

Mass sickness.

Loved ones being taken and killed, with no way to protect them.

Epic failure.

Dread, shame, guilt, depression—Israel was spared none of it. The wrath of God was poured out on them, and poor Jeremiah was there to see it all. Imagine his heartache, pain, and torment. He not only experienced it with them but also knew it could have been prevented. All the pain and the sorrow could have easily been avoided if the people had just *listened* to what God had to say. In the middle of his despair, Jeremiah wrote:

> I remember my affliction and my wandering,
>> the bitterness and the gall.
> I well remember them,
>> and my soul is downcast within me.
> Yet this I call to mind
>> and therefore I have hope:
>
> Because of the LORD's great love we are not
>> consumed,
>> for his compassions never fail.
> They are new every morning;
>> great is your faithfulness.
> I say to myself, "The LORD is my portion;
>> therefore I will wait for him."

The LORD is good to those whose hope is in him,
to the one who seeks him. (Lam. 3:19–25)

From the worst of the pits, we hear sweet promises. The Jews who experienced the destruction were living out our worst fears. They faced loss, death, sickness, murder, poverty, and national turmoil. Their very home was desolate, they had no ways to protect their loved ones, and there was no end to their pain in sight.

Yet *this* I call to mind, and therefore we *all have hope*:

- Because the Lord loves us, we will not be consumed.
- God's compassions will *never* fail us.
- Every single morning we awake with new hope.
- God's faithfulness is *great*.
- The Lord is our portion, and he *will* provide.
- When we wait for him, he will come.
- The Lord is good to those who hope in him.

We know and can be assured that even *if* our worst fears come true, we have hope, compassion, faithfulness, newness, and provision from a God who does not lie to us.

Do you see, then, what happens to the ideas that our fears are based on? They are disarmed. They are calmed. They go from causing raging pain in our minds to a side thought in the back of our minds. Our fears get demoted. They get fired from being allowed to rule us, and we and our unwavering faith take on the role of ruling over *them*.

You see, our fears are not trustworthy. They are not based on truth, they do not know facts, and they are guilty of vast exaggeration. Our fears do not love us, they do not care for us, they take no account of our pain or our sorrow. Our fears are unworthy of our attention. They do not deserve the deepest parts of us, nor do they deserve our attention or our allegiance.

Instead, we offer our attention and our allegiance to God, who is trustworthy, who is truth, and whose promises are real. Our fears loom over us, in dark shadows and scary places. We imagine them large and unbeatable, yet we never turn around to actually *look at them*. In this process of facing them and sizing them up, we realize how small they are in comparison to the greatness that is ours through Christ. Once we gaze upon our fears with honest indignation, we can see that, yes, God is bigger than even the worst thing we can imagine.

> Our fears are not trustworthy. They are not based on truth, they do not know facts, and they are guilty of vast exaggeration.

When I was in the middle of one of my worst days, each minute felt like a year. I didn't have enough strength or pain stamina to make it through the next sixty seconds, never mind the next weeks or months. I did not yet have the truth I am sharing with you; instead, I was living in the middle of consuming fear. I was in it; it loomed large, and I saw no way out. I needed rescuing; I needed the hope and the faithfulness and the provision that the book of Lamentations speaks about. Everything hurt. I was five months pregnant with a baby I knew was not going to live, and pain resonated out of places I did not even know I had.

This is what I wrote:

I just can't find you, Lord! You feel distant, a whisper in the wind, when I feel like I need an up close, loud, and strong lion. I am wearied from this sadness and journey, yet I know you continue to call me to trust you. To walk blindly with you leading me, even though I do not know where you are taking me. Each minute feels like an hour, and each day feels like a year. How am I going to make it through this, Lord?

Then *this* is what I heard, and peace that saved my life flooded like a tidal wave:

My sweet one, in the whispers of your soul I am here. Do not be afraid to listen, to hear me, and to believe. I will *not* let you down. Though the circumstances of this life and the hardness of your days tempt you to think I don't love you, you know that I do. I have promised you that I will never leave you, and I won't. I love your sweet baby Gideon. O how I love him and desire great things for my children. His life, it is not a tragedy, though I know that you think it is. His life, it is not sad, for it is eternal. Your baby, your precious Gideon, is helping me to make all things new in you. He is my worker, my precious child whom I have chosen to bring you through this. This is what *life* truly is. It is not of this world! It is not of these days, it is not in the pleasures or distractions you experience. It is with *me*. Only *me*. Do not be afraid of the days to come; though you cannot see or know the details, you can see and know that I will be in *all* of them. Not one is out of my reach.

Friends, those words are not of this world. For there is a greater power at work in us than we can even begin to comprehend. This power is ours through Christ and lives in us through the Holy Spirit and gives us hope. Those words penetrated my heart and my spirit, and I got up off the floor, wiped away my tears, and somehow lived in a miraculous joy despite the pain, fear, and sorrow. The miraculous joy is for you too.

So What Are We Talking About?

By answering the question "What is your greatest fear?" we already called it out by name. Now it is time to ask why. *Why* is that thing, or that scenario, or that loss, or that death something that grips us so much?

Our fears tell us something about our faith. Our fears highlight and illuminate the areas we honestly do not believe God's power can touch. It's not something we like to admit and definitely never *ever* say out loud. But if we want to live free from our fears, we have to first identify what it is we are actually fighting against. It is lack of faith. Not lack of faith in God entirely, but lack of faith in him over certain aspects of our lives.

My husband and I both struggle with fear, but we are as different in our fear as two can possibly be. Dave never spent much time worrying about losing a child; fear of death or losing someone does not grip him. Of course, he loves our children as much as I do, so why wouldn't he fear losing them? After all, his own wife lost sleep over the idea. It is because when he plays out the scenario in his mind, when he dissects the idea of losing a child, the conclusion is always the same to him: heaven. My husband, Dave, has a strong and excited outlook on heaven. He always has. Dave's passion about heaven and his accurate treatment of its magnificence have always been a part of his faith that I deeply admire. So, to him, why spend time fearing something that you know ultimately ends well?

Me? Three years ago you could not have gotten me to even utter those words out loud. Even with my deep belief in God and my trust in his Word, I always avoided the topic of heaven. It scared me to think about death; I just didn't want to. Heaven didn't really sound better to me than holding my child in my arms. So when fears and worries flooded me, I had no faith-filled answer! I wanted hope, but I had nowhere to place it. I always rationalized and said, "Believing in the real-life, awesome place of heaven is just not my spiritual strength." Baloney. That excuse kept me fearing *deeply* for years. The dissection of my fear revealed to me a vast lack of trust in what the Bible says about heaven.

Okay, but what about Dave? It's nice that he gets to skip the tormenting fear of the death of a loved one. But what is *his* deal? Fear of failing is what keeps Dave up at night.

Oftentimes during our date nights, Dave will bring up something along these lines: "What if I should be doing something else for a living? What if I'm failing at being who I am supposed to be? What if I fail at being a dad? Are we missing something at being parents? What should we be doing better? What areas of our family need improvement?" The ins and outs of these questions stir mercilessly in his mind, and worry and anxiety take hold of his thinking. Dave's fear of failure comes down to one word: control.

At Gideon's graveside, Dave shared his struggle with anxiety with our family and friends. It went something like this:

> I never thought I would be able to stand here. When we first found out that Gideon was not going to live, I thought, *I cannot have a funeral for my baby. I cannot stand next to a little baby casket.* But I can stand here today and tell you that I would not change a minute of it. God has taught me so much through Gideon's life, and trusting in God during this season has brought me more peace than I ever felt possible. I always worried about small things, wanting control over everything; if I couldn't have complete control over something, I became anxious. Gideon's life changed all that. I trust God to be in control. I see that he is worthy of my trust, and now when those anxious thoughts come, I remember Gideon, and I do not dwell on them anymore.

Truth be told, Dave trusted in his own ability over God's ability. When something became out of his full control or full ability, Dave panicked. Clearly, God cannot pick up the pieces of *this*! In full dissection of Dave's deepest fear, these questions arose: Do you trust God more than you trust yourself? Do you trust him to guide you and not lead you astray? Can you give him blind trust and blind control?

Now you, friend, why do you fear what you fear? What does it reveal to you about your belief in God or his Word? There is freedom on the other side of these questions, I promise! As someone who has journeyed down the deep path of these questions and come out on the other side, I sit here with confidence and tell you: hope comes. Yes, it is ugly at first. Fears are ugly. The circumstances that surround our fears are ugly. Even the thought of going through them is sobbing-ugly-tears-type ugly. But what is uglier is continuing to let them live in darkness. Together, may we seek the truth about *why* we fear, and may we allow God to reveal in us those areas in which our faith needs to increase.

Your Journey

I pray that you will take courage. I pray that as you take time to reflect on what you fear and why you fear it, you will remember that God does not leave us nor forsake us. God will meet you in your time of reflection. Will you give him that chance? I know it is not fun to stare your fears in the face, but my prayer for you is that it might be less scary than you imagine. I pray that as you go forward, you will see how marvelously God makes up for our weaknesses. Though we may cower in fear and trembling, God is there in all his glory to lift us up.

Father, as we enter into this time with you, I pray that you will help us to see our fears the way you see them. I pray that you will leave nothing hidden, will lay bare before us the truth about our fears, and will bring hope! I pray that though it might be unbearable at first, we will allow you the chance to come work in us. I pray that you will give us the strength to be honest, to be detailed, and to leave nothing uncovered. Will you be our great teacher? Will you show us the lies behind our fears? Will you show us where we have traded in your hope for our distorted view of circumstances? Lord, will you meet us gently in this way? We know you are loving and gentle. We also know you are powerful, and I pray that your limitlessness might be proven to us. That as we seek you, we will find you, and that you will show us the faith we need to have hope! Hope despite our fears! Father, we trust you. Help us now to make these words come alive. It is in the powerful name of Jesus that I pray. Amen.

Questions for Reflection

1. What does your greatest fear look like? From beginning to end, what would it look like if it unfolded before you?

2. What do you think would happen to your faith if something bad, difficult, or terrible came into your life?

3. As you unpack your fear, do you imagine God being there? In what ways do you imagine him there? In what ways do you leave him out of the story?

4. If the worst did happen, do you think your faith would grow stronger or weaker? Write down all the ways you would choose to trust (or maybe not trust) God. Be honest with him. Just how big do you really believe God is?

5. In the midst of your pain or your fear, what do you need from him? Do you believe he could provide it?

6. Right now, what details about your life can you give over to him?

7. What do you hear God saying to you? If you feel brave enough, write down what you hear him saying.

8. Will you pray these words over your life?

> I lift up my eyes to the mountains—
> where does my help come from?
> My help comes from the LORD,
> the Maker of heaven and earth.
>
> He will not let your foot slip—
> he who watches over you will not slumber;
> indeed, he who watches over Israel
> will neither slumber nor sleep.
>
> The LORD watches over you—
> the LORD is your shade at your right hand;
> the sun will not harm you by day,
> nor the moon by night.

The LORD will keep you from all harm—
    he will watch over your life;
the LORD will watch over your coming and going
    both now and forevermore. (Ps. 121)

5

Wrestling Matches
with God

I'm not one of those "good" Christians.

I'm not one of those believers in Jesus who heard a fatal diagnosis for their baby and just accepted it. I'm not one of those churchgoers who would not even consider ending my pregnancy early. Nope, I'm not one of them. I wish I was. I wish I was brave enough to have made the decision to carry Gideon straight out of the gate. But I'm not. And I didn't. I wrestled with God over it, and I wrestled him *hard*.

I told you that I had the choice, and it was awful. I wish I'd never had the choice. I wish that the option to be in control had never been given to me. I wish that Gideon was just going to come when he was going to come and that was that. Having the option to take control was alluring, tempting— and awful.

Isn't that just it? Isn't that the basis of so many of our fears? We have just enough control to make us feel as if we are the ones who *are in control*. We have just enough choices, just enough options, just enough ideas so as to live fully in the illusion that we have control. Trouble is, we were not created for control. We were created for submission to our kingly leader. But the second that fruit was bitten, the knowledge of good and evil came, and the fight for control began.

News flash: any sense of control we have is an illusion.

If I can just control my job performance, then maybe I will never lose my job.

If I can just feed my children the right foods and never feed them out of plastic containers that have been in the microwave, then my children will not get cancer.

If I can just keep enough money in the bank, then we will never have financial issues.

If I can just please everyone around me, then I will always be liked and popular.

If I can just keep to a certain amount of calories per day and hit up my Burn Bootcamp class three mornings out of the week, then I will always have good health.

If I can just please my spouse enough, then they will never leave me.

If I can just put my household on a good schedule, keep the house perfectly spotless, and make only home-cooked meals, then I will be a good wife and mother.

All of it? It's a lie. We know that it is, and *that* is why we fear so much. Deep down we know we are not in control, and we hate it. But the truth is that our "out of controlness" is really the greatest gift God could ever give to us. He is far better at being God than we are, but because he loves us so much, he meets us in our waywardness. He *wants* us to wrestle with him. God wants us to bring to him, full force, all that we want to have control over. He wants to hear our moans, our complaints, and our opinions, and in these meetings, he wants to show off his splendor.

When God Shows Off

I told you that Gideon did not come early. I told you that I went to the hospital and the medicine didn't take. What I didn't tell you was how God intervened in the middle of my control.

Yes, we have choices. Yes, God allows us (for the most part) the honor of choosing where we live, what job we have, how many children we birth, what kind of friends we keep, where we go on vacation. But even in our control, there is beauty in full surrender. When we surrender, God intervenes when we need him most. And when we live needing him most, isn't that where true joy and peace really exist? This fact and assurance should bring us great peace: even in our wandering God does not leave us.

This fact reminded me of the Israelites after Moses parted the Red Sea. You would think that those people would never have needed another act of God as long as they lived! But alas, they doubted God over and over again, even after God proved himself worthy of control over and over again.

I was like the Israelites. I needed multiple parting-of-the-sea moments.

I received a phone call at 2:35 a.m. the night before I was going to the hospital to end my pregnancy early. As the phone rang, I rolled over and thought, *I should answer that. God is calling.*

I did not know the woman on the other end of the line. She said her name was Jennifer, and she was calling to tell me all about her own baby son, James Asa. She had learned of our family's need for prayer in an email from a friend of a friend. She read our story, and she was compelled to call me.

I have often thought back to Jennifer's boldness. She didn't know me. She didn't know I was about to go into the hospital to bear my son early. She didn't even know what time zone I was in, hence her call at 2:35 a.m. But Jennifer had walked where I was now walking; she had lived through God's redemptive power. She could relate to my pain and simply obeyed the urge to call me. I thank God she did. Her phone call saved my life and gave more of a life to Gideon than I ever thought was possible.

The first thing she said to me was, "You don't know me, but I also had a baby with Potter's Syndrome. Would you mind if I told you my story?" Then she uttered the words that were my first glimmer that God was in full control and was calling me to carry Gideon. She said, "James Asa lived for two hours. I would not trade anything in the whole world for those moments I had with him. Holding him was the most precious time of my entire life."

I was confused. In my fear I believed that bearing Gideon would be hell on earth. I pictured a scene of suffering, one filled with death, and crying, and torment. I pictured myself crumbling under the pain a mother would feel as she ushered her child to heaven. I pictured nothing that I could handle.

Jennifer told a different story, and what began to unfold in my mind was that maybe, just maybe, God was bigger than my fears. Maybe, just maybe, God was asking me to do the impossible. Even though I clearly told him I could *not* survive it.

I asked Jennifer so many questions:

"You mean it wasn't awful?"

"You mean you don't lie awake in torment over watching your little baby die?"

"You mean your three older daughters survived holding and loving and meeting their little baby brother who was going to live in heaven?"

"You mean James Asa did not suffer?"

It was a middle-of-the-night miracle, a parting of the Red Sea, a God yelling at me loud and clear that he is in control and he is good at it. By the time I hung up the phone it was 4:00 a.m. I was due at the hospital at 5:30. As I lay my head back down onto the pillow, I whispered these words: "God, if you ask me to carry Gideon, I will do it." That night I experienced peace for the first time in weeks. That night I saw the first glimpse that God deserves the driver's seat of my life.

I wish I could tell you it was a one-night fix. My friend, that night was the first night of a one-month-long, all-out, almost-physical wrestling match. I am not joking with you. What I entered into with the Lord was as close to a physical fight as I think you can have. I fought him tooth and nail, but it was in the fighting that true surrender came.

God doesn't want our passive faith. He wants our active faith. Our very much honest and true and *fighting* faith. I did not like the fact that my baby was not going to live, and I told him *all* about it. What are you not happy about? Is there something today that you want to fight with God over? He is waiting for you. He wants to hear about it.

What Does Wrestling Look Like

We like being in control. We tell God with our lips that we trust him more, but our hearts are far from that truth. But you see, that is the problem. We are smart enough to know that there are many, many things out of our control, and fear begins. We attempt to keep control because we are more comfortable in that place, but we then notice that our power is limited. We can control only so much.

We have got to give it up. Not give it up kind of, sort of, or just for one day. No, we need to give it up entirely. We need to come to the complete and utter end of ourselves, take our death grip off of wanting control, and finally submit to the fact that God is simply better at being in control than we are.

In my mind, I picture a tug-of-war with God. We hand control over to him; we finally say, "Okay, Jesus! I trust you more than I trust myself. In *all things*, even the scary ones, I give you control." But we don't fully let go yet. We pull it back. "Well, on this one particular issue, can I have it back? Just for a second? I think I trust myself more on this one; you are not really moving fast enough for me." Then we try again. "Okay, okay, okay, fine. You proved faithful again, so here you go. You have the control back." We hand it back over, this time for a little longer. Until something scary comes along—a fearful thought, a crazy moment—and control feels better. "Last time, Jesus, I promise! I just need to take it back one more time."

Back and forth we go, until we come to the end of ourselves. Weary from the wrestling, we finally embrace God's full sovereignty over all things. He catches us as we collapse into his arms, tired of fighting with ourselves. He is waiting once more to be our Savior. That collapse—at the end, when you truthfully acknowledge and accept his control over all things, especially the fearful ones—feels so good. So freeing. For the first time, you finally allow yourself the freedom to admit that your fears are *not* in your hands. And you know what? It is well with your soul.

> Weary from the wrestling, we finally embrace God's full sovereignty over all things. He catches us as we collapse into his arms, tired of fighting with ourselves.

I'll never forget those days. It was Christmastime, and every day I would sit on my couch and stare at the tree. I would look at all the "Baby's First Christmas" ornaments and cry because Gideon would not have a first Christmas. I was frustrated with myself and with God. It had been weeks since my short stint in the hospital, weeks since I had seen God do actual miracles, and weeks since I had decided to carry Gideon to full term, but I was still so afraid. I thought that once I made the choice, I would feel better and just accept my path. I didn't, and every day I looked for ways to try to control the situation. In an uncontrollable circumstance, that is a very maddening thing to do. But, alas, I still tried.

Sitting on the couch one day, I pictured myself being like Jacob, wrestling with God all day and night trying to convince him to let me out of this situation. Do something, anything! Finally, on January 3, after weeks of fighting, I wrote the following verses in my journal:

> You hem me in behind and before,
>   and you lay your hand upon me.
> Such knowledge is too wonderful for me,
>   too lofty for me to attain. (Ps. 139:5–6)

Then I prayed these words:

I know you have me right where you want me, Lord. I finally believe it. Work on me, have your way with me. I only ask, Lord, that you have mercy on my sweet boy Gideon. Heal him, make him new . . . but whatever it is, may your will be

*done. Lord Jesus, I am learning what it means to rely on you
alone. In all that I have wrestled with, I pray for this time of
suffering I am in. In your name, I want to use it. May you
be enough for Gideon, may you be enough for me. Finally,
enough for me. Make straight my crooked path, one that
seems endlessly dark. Instead, make a short path, one that
leads straight into your compassionate and loving arms.*

The fight was over. I was finally ready to submit, and I
found that in the wrestling, Jesus and I had become closer
than we had ever been before. May the same be found by you.

Dwelling in God's Sovereignty

All her fear was wrapped up in control. My friend Ashley
was a self-proclaimed control freak, and it paralyzed her. As a
wife, a mother, and a friend, she tried to keep a tight grip on it
all. But in reality, *it all* had a tight grip on her. In our Breaking
the Fear Cycle class at church, she shared one day, with tears
in her eyes (which she hated because crying made her feel
out of control), "I have spent my whole life not wanting to
give God control. I wanted to keep it. I am finally realizing
that God's sovereignty over my life is *far better* than all of my
fearful controlling." Amen, sister.

There is power in this admission. It might come across as
just words, but something happens in our spirits and we are
humbled when we simply talk to God and tell him that we believe he is worthy of control. God is capable and trustworthy,

but he is not forceful. He will not force his way into control; we must hand it over to him.

Praise God that he has left us his wisdom. We have pages and pages full of God's advice in his Word on how to actually accept his sovereignty over our lives. Will you dig into Proverbs 3 with me for a moment?

Step 1: Do Not Forget His Teaching

> My son [or daughter], do not forget my teaching,
>> but keep my commands in your heart,
> for they will prolong your life many years
>> and bring you peace and prosperity. (vv. 1–2)

Take care of his words and keep them in your heart. Adore the Bible the way you adore that latest bestseller or the next Nicholas Sparks story. Taste and see that throughout history God has never failed. Never. But we need a constant reminder of this. In order to regularly embrace God's control over our lives, we need to be constantly reminded that he is powerful and worthy of such a role in our lives.

Did you hear? It is God's commands that will bring peace and prosperity. It is in them *alone* that peace and prosperity will come.

Step 2: Be in Control of You

> Let love and faithfulness never leave you;
>> bind them around your neck,
>> write them on the tablet of your heart.

> Then you will win favor and a good name
> in the sight of God and man. (vv. 3–4)

We are fidgety fearers; we must put our energy somewhere. When we so badly need/want to take control of something, we should take control of the one thing that is actually ours to control: our hearts. Why is it that we are constantly trying to exert our control over all that is external? Ironically, we pour our energy into the things that are not in our control and fully neglect the one thing that is. God's Word never offers us control over our families, our circumstances, our lives, or our hours. But he does offer us control over ourselves. May love and faithfulness be the mantra that we bind around ourselves. If we must be bound by something, may it be by God's Word! And then we will gain the very thing that our spirits so desperately crave: favor and a good name in the sight of God *and* man.

Step 3: Admit That Your Understanding Is Limited

> Trust in the LORD with all your heart
> and lean not on your own understanding;
> in all your ways submit to him,
> and he will make your paths straight. (vv. 5–6)

We think we know. We really do. I thought I knew what was best for me and my family. I really did. So did Ashley. So did Dave. I am sure you do too. In our limited and finite understanding, we really do believe that our own assessments are fully trustworthy. They are not. The thing is, God wants to actually *prove* this to us. I believe he delights in showing off in our lives and loves us enough not to keep us wondering whether his ways are better. God wants to make our paths straight, but this can happen only through our submission to him.

Step 4: Have an Accurate View of Self

> Do not be wise in your own eyes;
>   fear the LORD and shun evil.
> This will bring health to your body
>   and nourishment to your bones. (vv. 7–8)

We live in a time when having a high view of self is not only promoted but also considered essential to our sense of well-being. In the name of health and wealth, the world teaches us to lift ourselves high. If you think enough of yourself and your body, then you will be healthier—the best version of you! The Bible turns this ideal on its head. If we desire good health, the one we should be lifting up is God. If we are going to have a lofty view of anyone, may it be of the Lord himself. Then, in comparison to his very greatness, we will have to admit that we are not so wise after all! Our respect and reverence for God are what will bring lasting health and nourishment.

Chapter by chapter, verse by verse, God's Word proclaims his sovereignty! It is ingrained on every page and held high in every story. I am reminded over and over that there is *good reason* to hand over control to God.

I pray that you fall deeply in love with the Word of God

and not merely read it out of obligation or habit or "steps to being a good Christian." I pray that God's Word comes alive in you and takes hold of you. For his words are the *only* words that will make a lasting impact.

Will you come with me through the rest of these verses? It will be worth it; the ending is a great one.

> Honor the LORD with your wealth,
>> with the first fruits of all your crops;
> then your barns will be filled to overflowing,
>> and your vats will brim over with new wine.
>
> My son, do not despise the LORD's discipline,
>> and do not resent his rebuke,
> because the LORD disciplines those he loves,
>> as a father the son he delights in.
>
> Blessed are those who find wisdom,
>> those who gain understanding,
> for she is more profitable than silver
>> and yields better returns than gold.
> She is more precious than rubies;
>> nothing you desire can compare with her.
> Long life is in her right hand;
>> in her left hand are riches and honor.
> Her ways are pleasant ways,
>> and all her paths are peace.
> She is a tree of life to those who take hold of her;
>> those who hold her fast will be blessed.
>
> By wisdom the LORD laid the earth's foundations,
>> by understanding he set the heavens in place;

by his knowledge the watery depths were divided,
>   and the clouds let drop the dew.

My son, do not let wisdom and understanding out
>   of your sight,
>   preserve sound judgment and discretion;
they will be life for you,
>   an ornament to grace your neck.
Then you will go on your way in safety,
>   and your foot will not stumble.
When you lie down, you will not be afraid;
>   when you lie down, your sleep will be sweet.
Have no fear of sudden disaster
>   or of the ruin that overtakes the wicked,
for the LORD will be at your side
>   and will keep your foot from being snared. (vv.
>   9–26)

Did you see it? Please do not miss the gloriousness of this truth! It is God's promise that if we listen to him, if we take up his commands in our hearts, and if we trust his understanding over our own, then when we lie down, we will not be afraid. Tears come to my eyes as I realize that God sees us even when we sleep. He knows that our anxious hearts disturb our sleep and that we cannot find true rest. But through his wisdom there is rest. When we lie down, our sleep will be sweet.

I want sweet sleep. Don't you?

Write these verses on your heart and implant them on your mind, for verse 25 tells us that we do not need to fear sudden disaster. Not tsunamis, terrorism, earthquakes, political unrest, shootings, and so on. Those who do not fear God fear these things. Not us. We have been set apart, and we have been armed. For the Lord *will* be at our side. He *will*.

Your Journey

It is no small thing to come to the end of yourself. It makes you feel vulnerable, is humbling, and takes a lot of courage. I believe you are already brave. You can do this. Can you hand over all the things you hold on to so tightly? Would you be brave and open up your hands and release to a God who is waiting the things in your life that you keep a white-knuckled grip on? There are not many things I know for sure in this life and there are not many promises I can make for certain, but this I can tell you with confidence: God will take good care of them all. As you spend time with God, processing with him, may you allow this prayer to wash over you.

Father, will you forgive us? We have been blind for too long and have held up our ways as so high and lofty. We confess that we do not understand as you do. We admit that we are not as wise as you are. We claim that your goodness far surpasses our own, and we ask that your Holy Spirit will come now and be our guide. God, will you reveal in us the areas in which we take control away from you? Will you show us the places where you want to relieve us of that responsibility? I pray that you will show off your power!

Please bless my sisters and brothers who so desperately desire sweet sleep and long-lasting peace. I pray for a complete power change. Not a one-minute change or a one-day change; I pray for a life change. That every day we will once more hand over control to you. That you will give us your wisdom to recognize when we are tempted to take it back. Thank you, Lord, for your Word, which does not leave us stranded but gives us tangible wisdom and direction. May it come alive in our hearts once more! May we turn to you often and sincerely. And may we confess now with our mouths that you are good, you are holy, you are powerful, and you are worthy of all our trust. Come now, Lord. In Jesus's name, I pray. Amen.

Questions for Reflection

1. What are some things in your life that you desperately try to keep control of?

2. Are you willing to give these things to God and let him have control over them instead? Why or why not?

3. What are some reasons why you are afraid of letting go of control? Will you talk to God about these things?

4. As a symbol of giving God control, get a few small pieces of paper. On each one, write down something you try to keep in your control. Is it finances? Your

job? A friendship? A marriage or the desire for marriage? A child or the desire for a child? Take time one by one to pray and give them over to God's control. When you are finished, fold each one and write on it "Surrendered to God" along with the date. Keep them in a prominent place where you can see them and re-surrender them to God as often as you need to.

6

Believing in the Bible's View of Suffering

I get it. Who likes pain? In fact, we have been raised, taught, and enabled to virtually live without it.

Avoid pain at all costs! Happy happy, joy joy, do what makes you feel good, you can do whatever you put your mind to, and prosperity for all!

Pain at the dentist? No problem. Take Novocain and
  laughing gas.
Pain in your back? No problem. Grab some pain meds.
Pain in your heart? No problem. Head to a counselor.
Pain in your mind? No problem. Time heals all wounds.
Pain over losing someone? No problem. God must have
  needed another angel.

What has happened to us? We have taken any and all sources of pain and come up with some way to try to make the pain go away. We don't like to talk about death, we don't like to acknowledge the hard things, and we most assuredly want to avoid pain at all costs. Think about it. Drill down to the very bottom of every single one of your fears, and you will find the same thing: pain.

We know that not all pain can be medicated, surgically removed, or fixed. In the deepest parts of us, we understand that pain cannot be avoided; so we fear because we don't have an answer for it.

We are an abundantly fearful people. Why? We have more comfort and peace than most people in all of history. This thought often brings me back to a trip to Rome, Italy, when I was thirteen years old. I stood in the Colosseum and recalled all that had taken place there. I imagined what it was like for the people who stood in those stands, and I shuddered in terror at what it was like for the people standing behind that gate. Their lives were about to end in an awful way. Whole families would be standing there—mothers, fathers, children—the Colosseum had no mercy. There were no rules, no laws for protection, surely no medicine that could take away the pain of it all. Would we be able to survive even a single minute if we were born in a different period in history? A different part of the world?

It might sound silly, but I often use this example in my mind. When fears pop into my mind, when irrationality starts to flow, I think to myself, *At least I'm not standing behind those Colosseum doors, babies in hand, no way to protect them.*

At least I'm not there. It may sound crazy, but doing so helps me to center my thinking. It brings me back to the origin of my fear and reminds me how far I have come from what the Bible actually says about pain.

Pain is not bad. Not at all.

When I was pregnant with Gideon, I felt as though I were standing in an unquenchable fire, and no matter which way I turned, I couldn't get out of it. I tried to run away with all my might. I would back up and take a running leap, only to hit a wall that bounced me right back into the pain. I kept turning to God about this.

God, why won't you let me get out of this?

Maria, why are you trying so hard to run away from the pain?

Because it hurts! It's pain and it hurts and I want out!

Maria, pain is not a bad thing. It's what I am here for. I am here to stand with you in the pain, not to get you out of it.

There it was. So there I stood, finally accepting that the pain was not mine to avoid. The pain was there for me to sit in and endure. But I was not trained for this. In my mind, pain equaled bad and no pain equaled good. I was not armed for the battle because my mind had gotten so far from the truth.

If we can together, even slightly, begin to dig into the truth and discover the value of pain, perhaps we can gain freedom from some of our fear. If we can attain a healthy perspective on pain, maybe we can combat our tendency to fear it.

A handful of books have changed my life through the years. Nancy Guthrie's book *Be Still, My Soul: Embracing God's Purpose and Provision in Suffering* is one of them. In this compilation of writings on the topic of suffering, I found much hope in Philip Yancey's excerpt from his book with Dr. Paul Brand, *The Gift of Pain*. He explains that though we see pain in negative terms, physical pain has a job to do, warning our bodies of illness and danger. Yancey uses the role of physical pain in our lives to help explain the role of mental, emotional, and spiritual pain. That pain also carries a purpose. I've clung to the following words in particular many times:

> Pain, God's megaphone, can drive me away from faith. I can hate God for allowing such misery. Or, on the other hand, it can drive me to God. I can believe the promise that this world is not all there is, and take the chance that God is making a perfect place for those who follow him on pain-wracked earth.[1]

Pain is actually doing something. It is not arbitrary, worthless, or endless. It's doing a work in us that cannot be done any other way. Do I believe that God took joy over the death of my sweet Gideon? No, absolutely not. Do I believe that tragedy, sickness, and death are part of the evils of this world? Yes, absolutely. But because we have a good, loving, merciful, and *powerful* God, he takes what is bad and makes it do *his* work.

Will you learn with me? Can we, for just a few pages, set aside both what we think we know about pain and our self-defense mechanism of pain avoidance and dive into what the Bible says about our pain?

The Bible Verses We Like to Skip Over

Anytime something bad happens to someone, what is the first Bible verse that comes to mind? Come on, you know it. Say it with me, all together now, "And we know that in all things God works for the good of those who love him, who have been called according to his purpose" (Rom. 8:28).

It's such a lovely verse. It feels so nice to say and surely gives us hope in times of trouble. But if I've learned anything about Scripture, it is this: we do a vast disservice to God's Word when we pluck out verses and have them stand alone. We do this for our convenience and to make us feel better rather than for the sake of truth. But *truth* is our only hope.

Let's back up a little to Romans 8:18. It's one of those verses to implant in our minds and bring out when we are afraid. Paul says, "I consider that our present sufferings are not worth comparing with the glory that will be revealed in us." And what are the sufferings he's referring to? Paul lists them for us in 2 Corinthians 11:24–28:

> Five times I received from the Jews the forty lashes minus one. Three times I was beaten with rods, once I was pelted with stones, three times I was shipwrecked, I spent a night and a day in the open sea, I have been constantly on the move. I have been in danger from rivers, in danger from bandits, in danger from my fellow Jews, in danger from Gentiles; in danger in the city, in danger in the country, in danger at sea; and in danger from false believers. I have labored and toiled and have often gone without sleep; I

have known hunger and thirst and have often gone without food; I have been cold and naked. Besides everything else, I face daily the pressure of my concern for all the churches.

Yet, Paul knew that pain does a work in us, an eternal work. Every time we hurt, every time we cry, every time pain is too much to bear, it still cannot be compared to the eternal glory that God is weaving into our souls. The pain will last for a night, but the glory will last forever.

I know it is tempting to let those words roll right off you, to hear them as "blah, blah, blah, that sounds nice but it doesn't really help." I was that way too. All the talk of suffering and glory just made me want to curl up and shut down. But that's exactly why we need to talk about it, because the part of me that wanted to shut down was the same part that created all my fears. Doubt welled up and fear took over. We have to find something greater than our temporary lives to grab on to; there has got to be more.

Paul gives us more in Romans 8:19–21:

The creation waits in eager expectation for the children of God to be revealed. For the creation was subjected to frustration, not by its own choice, but by the will of the one who subjected it, in hope that the creation itself will be liberated from its bondage to decay and brought into the freedom and glory of the children of God.

This world, left to itself, will decay. This is why our rational thinking results in fear. Fear really does make sense. We live in a world that is in bondage to decay. Who wouldn't fear? We are set up for failure, pain, and loss. "Creation was subjected to frustration"—we will strive toward perfection, safety, and happiness, but we will be left frustrated, unable to grasp what we strive for, because they don't exist. But we will be liberated! We will be free. We will be glorious. For we are children of God.

As for now? As for these days?

> We know that the whole creation has been groaning as in the pains of childbirth right up to the present time. Not only so, but we ourselves, who have the firstfruits of the Spirit, groan inwardly as we wait eagerly for our adoption to sonship, the redemption of our bodies. For in this hope we were saved. But hope that is seen is no hope at all. Who hopes for what they already have? But if we hope for what we do not yet have, we wait for it patiently. (vv. 22–25)

I think it might be time for us to change our expectations. Instead of living in perpetual fear of the pain and suffering that *might happen*, let's live each day in *freedom*. It's as though we are tiptoeing through a minefield, praying and pleading with every step, "Please, God! Don't let me explode! Help me not to step on one of the mines!" The fact is the entire world blew up a long time ago. Paradise as God intended it was lost when sin and death entered in. But God has given us the tools to walk freely and without fear.

In verse 23, Paul reminds us that we have the firstfruits of the Holy Spirit. The very Spirit of God who raised Jesus from the dead also lives in us and gives comfort, wisdom, power, and counsel. We also have the redemption of our bodies. There is nothing that happens in this lifetime that heaven cannot heal.

In verses 24–25, we learn that we have hope. We are saved! But who hopes for what he already has? If we currently had the perfection, contentment, money, safety, and guarantees that we strive for, what, then, would be the purpose of heaven? No, instead we wait for those things patiently. (Far more often, we don't wait patiently but rather fear and beg and plead with God for them. That is why we are going through this book together!)

There is still more:

> In the same way, the Spirit helps us in our weakness. We do not know what we ought to pray for, but the Spirit himself intercedes for us through wordless groans. And he who searches our hearts knows the mind of the Spirit, because the Spirit intercedes for God's people in accordance with the will of God. (vv. 26–27)

We are not meant to muscle through our fear on our own. Because we are weak, we are not able to conquer it, beat it, and get rid of it. We are not yet home in heaven; suffering will be a part of these days. But together we take heart. We don't need words or understanding; we need only to rely on the Spirit in us. God does not say we should desire pain and suffering. He only expects us to acknowledge his goodness and his plan and to allow his Spirit in us to do the rest. We don't even know what to ask for! We don't have to. God searches our hearts, he knows our minds, and the Holy Spirit does the good work of asking for what we truly need.

Now, only *now*, do we come to Romans 8:28. Only *after* all that! After our acceptance of suffering, our acknowledgment of our eternal hope, our admittance of our weakness, only after God searches our hearts, minds, and needs, then and only then does God work all things for good. God working all things for good is not magic pixie dust that makes everything nice and pretty; it is a promise that reminds us of the good work he desires to do in and through us, pain and all.

I could live in Romans 8. If I didn't stink at memorizing Scripture, I would memorize the entire chapter. It is so wonderfully complex and hope filled. My prayer for you as you read these verses is that you will allow each word to soak into your spirit. That you would put on your fear filter and see how these words can bring freedom from fear. Take each word, don't leave even one out, and see what God does in your soul.

The Marriage of Fear and Pain

My daughter is one of those "lucky" ones prone to strep throat. She will wake up with tears in her eyes because she knows what's coming. Little white spots on her throat, slight fever, pain when she swallows, and Mommy on the phone scheduling her appointment. Then comes the wave of fear over the dreaded throat swab.

"Mommy, it's going to hurt!"

Here we go again. We are on throat swab appointment number 568 and still the same thing.

"But, honey," I say, "doesn't your throat hurt already? Don't you want the medicine that will make it go away?"

"Yes, but I don't want the throat swab! I'm scared!"

Fourteen Beanie Boos, two nurses, and one throat swab later, the medicine finally kicks in and she is good to go. The dreaded twelve hours of fear and crying before the appointment are always inevitably much worse than the two-second throat swab.

What gives? Can she not please, oh, pretty please, spare us the moaning and just remember that it is going to be okay? Can she not read chapter 6 of Mommy's book and just trust that it will be all right? It's always easier said than done.

This marriage of fear and pain has a deep hold on us, and we know nothing else to do *but* fear the pain. It doesn't have to be this way. It doesn't have to keep a hold on us. When we can take a deep breath, think rationally, and recognize that our fear is about pain, we can begin to battle the fear with Scripture and truth.

> 1 Peter 4:12: "Dear friends, do not be surprised at the fiery ordeal that has come on you to test you, as though something strange were happening to you."
>
> *Truth*: Pain should not take us by surprise.

John 16:33: "In this world you will have trouble. But
take heart! I have overcome the world."

Truth: We will have pain in this life, but God rules over
all.

1 Peter 5:10: "And the God of all grace, who called you
to his eternal glory in Christ, after you have suffered
a little while, will himself restore you and make you
strong, firm and steadfast."

Truth: Pain can make us strong.

James 1:2–3, 12: "Consider it pure joy, my brothers
and sisters, whenever you face trials of many kinds,
because you know that the testing of your faith pro-
duces perseverance.... Blessed is the one who perseveres under trial because, having stood the test, that
person will receive the crown of life that the Lord
has promised to those who love him."

Truth: Pain can bring us joy.

It is going to be okay.

We are going to be okay. You are going to be okay. We
can do this.

In retrospect, you want to know what bothered me
most from my time carrying Gideon? After experiencing
what true suffering and pain felt like, I was so angry that I
had wasted so many painless days in fear. I was so mad at
myself for making up fires in my brain. My friend, if you

are in a time of suffering in your life, I pray that you find encouragement through the endurance of many brothers and sisters in Christ who have come before you. If you are not in a time of suffering, I pray that you will learn from my mistakes. Do not waste your moments in fear. Do not spend one precious moment of joy focusing on fear of pain; if and when the pain does come, God will be there in unimaginable ways.

About six months after Gideon died, my deep grief began to pass. I felt that the hardest days of mourning were behind me, and I sensed that God was calling me out of the hurt. The pain was like standing in unquenchable fire, hurt on every side, and for a time, I simply had to endure it. At the six-month mark, I imagined I had finally reached the end of burning. I sprinted as fast as I could until I broke free entirely from the flames. When I reached clean air, I paused to look back at them. *Am I really out? Is it really time for the pain to come to an end?* I felt a sense of relief, joy, and excitement that I had survived, and I remember feeling so *new*—whole, beautiful, and wonderful! As if a new me emerged from the flames. God did that. God did that through Gideon. God did that through the pain. He made something wonderful and new in me. The fire was worth it. Here's why.

We all say we want greatness. We all dream of being a part of something amazing. We even pray to see miracles in our

> Do not spend one precious moment of joy focusing on fear of pain.

lifetimes. God does all these things *in us* when we turn to him in times of deep pain. If I hadn't gone through the fire myself, I wouldn't have believed it. But now, I wish someone had convinced me to remember that I serve a *powerful God*. I serve a *supernatural God* who has armies and powers unseen. I serve a *generous God* who has paradise awaiting me in heaven. In the day-to-day, everyday, and pain-free moments of life, it is easy to forget that this is the God in whom we trust. Yes, God brings us through pain, and afterward, we remember and live in the truth that there is *nothing* our God cannot do.

But *how* does God do this in us?

He gently teaches us.

In the pain of losing a child, God taught me to hold more loosely to the days of this world.

In the pain of carrying a baby I knew would not live, God taught me that what he says is vastly more trustworthy than the words of every expert and doctor combined.

In the pain of watching my children hurt, God taught me that he can be trusted to take care of my children.

In the pain of wondering how I would survive each day, God sent messages of love and encouragement through friends and family in the form of cards, meals, and gifts.

In the pain of feeling alone in my hurt, God sent me stories of hope and redemption through women who had walked the same road.

In the pain of having to walk into a doctor's office every
  month full of happy and healthy pregnant women,
  God sent me a doctor who offered me a private en-
  trance and waiting room and who treated me with
  overwhelming compassion.

In the pain of making the hardest decision of our lives,
  God provided us with our amazing pastor and friend
  Mitch, who walked with us hand in hand.

In the time I am in now, the season after the suffering, fear
of pain still comes for me. I fear the pain of losing again, I
fear the pain of failing, and I fear the pain of judgment. But
when it comes, I remember how God draws close in pain
and how he uses pain. Then my thinking goes something
like this:

1. Am I fearing something I know to be true? No.
2. Am I fearing something that could come true? Well,
   yes.
3. If it does come true, can I trust God to comfort me?
   Yes.
4. Do I believe that God can use pain and meet me in
   it? Yes.
5. Then can I trust God with this fear and let it go? Yes.

Sometimes I ask myself question number one and the
fear subsides there. Sometimes I have to ask myself all five
questions, but hope and calm always come.

Your Journey

It is no small thing to bring our view of the Bible into question. But it is a question I believe we must ask ourselves. As we go into this section of self-reflection, I pray that you will put on the lens of pain. How do you address pain—physical, emotional, mental, and financial—in your life? What is your initial reaction to even the word *pain*? There is a digging up even of our childhood when we address these questions, and I pray for the courage you need to allow yourself to go there.

In this section in particular, I challenge you to be okay with asking the hard questions. Why does God allow pain? Is a God who allows pain a good God? Why wouldn't he choose to spare us from pain entirely? Take these questions to God; don't allow them to control you. Give them over to him, seek godly and biblical wisdom, and allow God to reveal his answers to you. God is not afraid of our questions, nor does he punish us for asking them. He knows our questions and our hearts, and he desires to teach us more. When we think some questions are too horrible to ask, dark places of fear come. So ask them. Trust me, God is a reliable friend. We can go to him with *all* our deepest and darkest fears, thoughts, and questions.

Maybe you don't want to be okay with pain. Understandably so. Maybe you feel that God is being unreasonable by asking us to find joy in our suffering. I felt that way once too; I just wasn't brave enough to admit it. When I read the Bible, I skimmed over those verses. I chose to ignore them. I pray that you will not.

Father, we come to you now and confess that sometimes we do not feel comfortable with your plan for pain. We would much rather be with you so that the groaning and the suffering and the pain would stop! We long for the perfection that your paradise will offer us someday. We dream of our tears being wiped from our eyes and a life of no more sickness and pain. This dream is in us; you put it there. It is a longing in us that draws us to you. But, Father, I pray that this desire in us would stop resulting in fear! I pray boldly that when fear of pain comes, you will give us a way out. May your Word bring us hope and a plan. May we acknowledge that the enemy has had a field day with our fear of pain. May you give us the strength and the courage to be honest with you instead and to confront the verses in your Word that scare us. Father, I pray that your Holy Spirit will come alongside us in this process. And when we do not have words, that your Spirit will intercede on our behalf. Search our hearts, know our minds, and call us forward to become more like you. I pray now that as we uncover the answers to the following questions, you will do a mighty work of peace in our lives. In Jesus's name, I pray. Amen.

Questions for Reflection

1. When you hear the word *pain*, what comes to mind? How does it make you feel?

2. Name some of your fears and the pain that comes with them. Can you give them over to God one by one in prayer?

3. Do you find it pure joy when you face trials of many kinds? Why or why not? Offer this question up to God. What do you hear him teaching you?

4. The verses throughout this chapter say that blessings come from trials. If this is true, why do we hate going through trials so much? Do you think you can allow your heart to find joy in hard times? How?

5. Do you have any tough questions for God about what his Word says in regard to suffering? Will you take them to him?

6. Which Bible verse about suffering gives you the most peace? Why?

7

Praying
Faith-Filled Prayers,
Not Fear-Filled Pleas

I never once believed Gideon was going to be healed.

Not once.

It was hard for me, then, when that is what everyone around me was encouraging me to pray for. I believed that God was more than capable of healing my baby. After all, the Bible is full of stories of God's miracles, and so is the radio! Yes, God *can* do it. But I did not believe he was going to this time.

How, then, was I to pray?

I was blessed with friends and family who prayed constantly for God to develop kidneys in Gideon. Our church prays over requests collected Sunday mornings, and every week I would read the same line submitted by Lindy, a dear friend of mine: "Please, God, please give Gideon kidneys!"

But how was *I* to pray when it felt more like begging than praying?

This question rolled over and over in my mind as I struggled with guilt over the fact that when I prayed for God to heal Gideon, it merely felt like lip service. This question brought back to my mind all the other similar-type prayers I had offered, most of them on a nightly basis:

> God, please bless my children, please keep them safe.
>
> Please protect my husband's job.
>
> Please let my child's fever go away *now*. Put your healing hand upon them.
>
> Please do not let any of my children ever participate in drugs or premarital sex, or make any mistakes of any kind ever. Thank you.
>
> Please give my kids great spouses. Prepare them even now, wherever they are, for my wonderful children.
>
> God, help me to decide if I should buy this new house/ car/TV.
>
> Please protect anyone I love from cancer, car accidents, mass shootings, and tsunamis.
>
> Please protect me from always looking like a hot mess! I just wish I could have it all together. Please help me to get it together.

I know these prayers might sound funny, but I promise you I have prayed every one of them, for real. Every night in my child's room I would rock them, wonder what on earth I should be praying for, and then come up with a laundry list full of begging and pleading. Then came the days when I was pregnant with Gideon—same room, same rocking chair, and my begging felt so futile. So wasteful of the little prayer energy I had in me.

So what then? If I am not praying for my laundry list of fear-based needs, what can I replace them with? When your fear list runs out because you finally give all your fears over to God (period), then what is there to talk to him about?

As I dug in, I found a level of praying I had never before discovered, a deeper layer of living life in prayer with God that lifted my spirit and my days. Amazing things happen when you spend time talking with God. I do want to preface this chapter by saying there is *nothing wrong with the begging prayers*. I believe God wants to hear all that is on our hearts. But if you are like me, a recovering fear-aholic, spending time praying about your fears is like putting a beer in an alcoholic's hand and telling them not to drink it. It is not helpful; instead, it tempts us to dig back into the fears that we spent so much time battling against.

God knows our fears. Rest assured he has heard me and you the first one thousand times we prayed for protection over our family and loved ones. He heard us, he knows, and we claim now his sovereignty over our lives. We remember that future telling is his job, and we give him control over our lives. He already understands us. I love how Emily Freeman touches on this sentiment in her book *Simply Tuesday*:

> I confess how disappointed I am that I don't have clarity. But in the confession, I begin to see Christ. I begin to release my obsession with building my life into something

linear, something I can figure out. Instead, I believe that letting go doesn't mean I'll be left with nothing. It means I can more fully hold on to Christ and trust in the life he is building within me. I sense him inviting me to trust him, not because I fully understand, but because I'll begin to believe he understands me.[1]

Our prayers are based in this trust. When we are confident, knowing full well that God already understands the depth of the desires of our hearts, we can be free to pray more boldly, more creatively, and more bravely. Let's learn how together.

How Jesus Prayed

No, this section is not about the Lord's Prayer.

I thought I had a very creative idea once (emphasis on *thought*). I was preparing to teach a ten-week class on prayer, and I thought, *Let's do a study looking at only the prayers that Jesus actually prayed in Scripture!* So off I went, digging through the four Gospels, expecting Jesus's many and eloquent prayers to easily fill up my Bible study. Wow, I clearly overestimated the times we actually *know* what Jesus prayed. I think we assume these texts are there because we know that Jesus prayed often. He constantly went away from his disciples to pray. Little did I realize we don't always get to hear *what* he prayed.

Excluding the Lord's Prayer (which I decided was Jesus teaching us *how* to pray and not necessarily what his own prayers sounded like), I found a scarce number of times

Jesus's prayers are recorded. So when we *do* get a backstage pass to listen to a conversation between Jesus and our heavenly Father, we should probably listen and take notes.

There Jesus was, about to die on the cross. Not only that, but everyone he loved—his friends, family, and even God himself—was about to turn their backs on him. Jesus was about to walk a road of pain and suffering like no one can ever imagine.

Let's look together at Jesus's last prayers and how we might model our prayers after his. May we take note and learn what the deeper-level prayer life looks like.

John 17:1–5

Jesus Prays for Himself

Father, the hour has come. Glorify your Son, that your Son may glorify you. For you granted him authority over all people that he might give eternal life to all those you have given him. Now this is eternal life: that they know you, the only true God, and Jesus Christ, whom you have sent. I have brought you glory on earth by finishing the work you gave me to do. And now, Father, glorify me in your presence with the glory I had with you before the world began.

A Prayer for Ourselves

Father, I come to you now in this season of life, and I ask that you will bring glory to me so that I might bring glory to you. You have brought me to this time and place as a woman or man, wife or daughter, mother or father, professional or at home, and I pray you will allow me to use the place I have in this life to bring others to you. May you finish the work in me that you gave me to do.

John 17:9–11, 15–16

Jesus Prays for His Loved Ones

I pray for them. I am not praying for the world, but for those you have given me, for they are yours. All I have is yours, and all you have is mine. And glory has come to me through them. I will remain in the world no longer, but they are still in the world, and I am coming to you. Holy Father, protect them by the power of your name, the name you gave me, so that they may be one as we are one. . . . My prayer is not that you take them out of the world but that you protect them from the evil one. They are not of the world, even as I am not of it. Sanctify them by the truth; your word is truth.

A Prayer for Our Loved Ones

I pray for those whom I love. You know those who are dearest to my heart, Lord. You have given them to me, and I thank you for them. All I have is yours, including those whom I love the most. They are yours, and I know you will care for them perfectly. I cannot be with them all the time and at every moment, but you are with them always. Holy Father, protect them by the power of your name so that they may be one with you! My prayer is not that you will save them from this world, but that you will protect them from the Evil One. They are not of this world, they are of your world, and I pray that you will sanctify them by the truth; your Word is truth.

John 17:20–23

Jesus Prays for All Believers

My prayer is not for them alone. I pray also for those who will believe in me through their message, that all of them may be one, Father, just as you are in me and I am in you. May they also be in us so that the world may believe that you have sent me. I have given them the glory that you gave me, that they may be one as we are one—I in them and you in me—so that they may be brought to complete unity. Then the world will know that you sent me and have loved them even as you have loved me.

A Prayer for Our Church

I pray not only for my dearest loved ones but also for your church. May we stand united in you. May we be one with one another just as we are one with you, Father, and your Holy Spirit who lives in us. May we remember that we have been given your glory and that you have given us all we need to serve in your name. May we do so together! Then the world will know that you sent Christ for us and that you love us even as you have loved him.

Matthew 26:38–39

Jesus Prays for His Fear

Then he said to [his disciples], "My soul is overwhelmed with sorrow to the point of death. Stay here and keep watch with me."

Going a little farther, he fell with his face to the ground and prayed, "My Father, if it is possible, may this cup be taken from me. Yet not as I will, but as you will."

A Prayer for Our Fear

Father, my soul is overwhelmed with sorrow to the point of death. The possibility of so many fearful things coming to pass in my life and the lives of my loved ones cripples me with dread. If it is possible, I pray that none of these things will happen. May the cup of pain pass over us. Yet not as I will, but as you will.

We are not Jesus, but we do have the presence of the living God within us, and it's through his power that we pray for the *greater things*. Jesus's prayers remind us that God is writing a larger story in our lives. So often, our fears take us inward. They suck us into the details of our lives, our families, our homes, our jobs, and our futures, and we forget that God's unfolding plan is so much bigger than the minute details of our lives. When we focus on our fears, we see only a tiny speck of the picture. Meanwhile, God is painting an entire mural that he desires us to be a part of. May we use our prayer time as an opportunity to take a step back and stop honing in on that one part of the picture that we find ourselves obsessing over. Take a step back in faith, and pray for God's *big* work to be done in us, in our lives, and in our churches.

I shudder when I think of all the work that would not have taken place had I ended my pregnancy early. If fear had had its way in me and Gideon had come on December 2 instead of March 31, entire stories and Bible studies and testimonies and *books* would not have been written! While I was focusing on the speck of time I found myself in, God was busy writing a greater story than I could have ever imagined.

I think of the woman who, after reading Gideon's story, decided to transport the grave of her tiny baby girl to the town where she now lives—a baby girl she had lost twenty years earlier.

I think of the family who confessed to me that they never fully grieved the loss of their little one and, after learning about Gideon, now celebrate the birthday of their child with balloons at their grave site.

I think of my husband, who could attend large social events only with Xanax in hand because of his anxiety and panic attacks. After Gideon came, he no longer struggled with anxiety in the way he once had. Those four months of pregnancy taught him what God can do in the face of struggle, and Dave lives so much freer now.

> While I was focusing on the speck of time I found myself in, God was busy writing a greater story than I could have ever imagined.

I think of my children. On December 2, my prayer was to protect them and shelter them from any and all pain. But they now see how good God is and how he walked them through the pain. They have less fear about bad things happening.

The list could go on forever. I won't get to see the full picture of God's working until I get to heaven. God has a mural in your life too, one he is working on daily. He wants to show you glimpses of his work. May your prayer time be an opportunity for God to show you what he is up to.

I wonder what the following list looks like for you.

Do you focus in so closely on wishing God would bless you at work with job security, a raise, or a new position, while he is working on a greater thing to be done in the lives of the people working around you?

Do you focus in so closely on praying for God to keep your children from harm, to keep them safe and happy, while God has the desire to grow their relationship with him, help them understand their spiritual gifts, and develop in them an amazing, godly character?

Does fear have you wrapped so tightly around your own thoughts and prayers that you cannot imagine God could use you to bless the lives of others and bring glory to his name through your words and actions?

Do you cling so fearfully to controlling every minute of your family's schedule that you have no time to pray at all? Or go to church? Or serve in a ministry?

Do you faithfully pray through a list of prayer requests, asking God to heal this person, help that person find a job, or this person get a house, or that person finally be blessed by a pregnancy and never once take the time to step back and ask God if you should reach out and minister to any one of them in person or with a phone call?

Please don't feel guilty. I know it is tempting to do so, but resist the fear rising up inside of you that you are not *good enough*. It's just the opposite. You are *so good* that God has more for you in your prayer life than what you believe you are capable of.

The Shift from Pleading to Praying

The war against fear in our lives begins in our minds, and it can end on the battlefield of prayer. We've been given a powerful weapon, yet we need training and instruction to wield it with precision and power. Chip Ingram shares:

> I urge you, then, as a matter of utmost importance, to be strong in the Lord. Stand firm and be alert. Gird yourself and use your weapons. Above all, pray. You represent the greatest army in all of history, and you fight for the greatest of causes. When the King comes in victory, you will receive the honors of a valiant warrior. And the invisible war will never need to be fought again.[2]

The battle over praying not pleading takes practice, but it is eternally worth engaging in. Some days, I would sit down to pray and draw a blank. I wanted to pray and not plead, but all that came to mind initially was more begging! It is a process and a discipline, but once mastered, it brings about great gains in our lives. And not only in our own lives but also in the lives of those around us.

Something happens when we take our prayers outward instead of inward. Fear subsides, and in its place a strong, generous person emerges, one so full of God's provision that we cannot help but want others to experience it too. Fear dissipates when those around us become more important than the fears within us.

In the beginning of this chapter, I gave you some examples of my own real-life pleas to God. Following are some examples of how I changed those pleas to prayers:

Plea for safety: God, please bless my children, please keep them safe.

Prayer for trusting in God: God, take care of my children in the way only you know how. I trust you with them fully.

Plea for security: Please protect my husband's job.

Prayer for good stewardship: God, I thank you for all you have provided for my family. I pray that you would help us to be good stewards of all you have entrusted to us.

Plea for healing: Please let my child's fever go away *now*. Put your healing hand upon them.

Prayer for healing: God, I know you are capable of all things. I pray for you to bring healing upon this child I love. I pray for your wisdom to know when and how to pray for healing, and I pray for the patience to trust in your timing.

Plea for perfection: Please do not let any of my children ever participate in drugs or premarital sex, or make any mistakes of any kind ever. Thank you.

Prayer for sanctification: I pray for my children to grow more and more in love with you. I pray that as they grow, you will prepare them and ready them, in your name, for all that life will bring to them. I pray that you will be there to comfort them when pain comes and that you will give them your wisdom to navigate all the valleys and the mountains of this life.

Plea for the future: Please give my kids great spouses. Prepare them even now, wherever they are, for my wonderful children.

Prayer for the future: I have no idea what the future will bring, Father. I pray that you will give me the courage to keep focused on today and only today. I give into your hands every detail of my children's futures. May you do a mighty work in their lives!

Plea for decision-making: God, help me to decide if I should buy this new house/car/TV.

Prayer for wisdom: Lord, I know you care most about my heart. I pray that in all things, you will give me the wisdom and the courage to set my heart first on you. Then, as I focus fully on you, may the smaller details in life come into clear focus.

Plea against tragedy: Please protect anyone I love from cancer, car accidents, mass shootings, and tsunamis.

Prayer in light of tragedy: God, this world is fallen, it is suffering, and many times it is scary. It seems like bad things are happening around every corner. You know that I desire to protect my loved ones from tragedy, but I commit now to trusting you in all things and at all times. I pray first for those in the midst of tragedy and ask you to comfort them and minister to them in a powerful and supernatural way. Lord, I pray for the courage not to fear tragedy, and I pray that you would prepare me and ready me if ever the day should come.

Plea for my image: Please protect me from always looking like a hot mess! I just wish I could have it all together. Please help me to get it together!

Prayer for God's glory: I recognize that you are made strong in my weakness and that I absolutely do not have it together outside of you. I pray for you to be glorified through my life and through my days. May all I say and do bring light to the amazing God you are, and when I fail, give me the courage to admit it and ask for forgiveness.

Your Journey

I understand there is almost something superstitious about praying against the things we fear the most. If we tell them to God often enough, maybe he won't let them happen to us. Like sports players who wear the same underwear for every game in hopes of always winning, we think we have to start and end our day praying through our list of fears. I pray constantly for you in this journey, that with each step you have the courage to pull off the Band-Aids that numb the fear from day to day. That you would, even now, have the boldness to take a break from praying against all that you fear, even if for only a day, a week, or a month. Don't pray about them. At all. No pleading to God to have him please, pretty please, not let your worst fears come true. Instead, talk to him about what he wants you to focus on.

Who would God like you to spend time loving on? In what ways might he desire to do work in and through you? What type of mural is he painting of your life? What *greater things* might he want you to consider?

As you enter into this time of taking a break from pleading, may I offer you the suggestion to keep your life free of fear triggers? It might mean staying away from the news, putting down magazines or certain types of books, or staying off social media altogether. It doesn't need to be a forever decision, but give yourself a goal of at least a week and see what difference it makes in your prayer life and in your fears.

I confess that once I took a break from the news and social media for the purpose of freeing my life of fearful praying, it was very hard to go back to them. I noticed that the space these things took up in my mind and my spirit was precious territory! Now I have good friends and family who keep me updated on the important things going on in the world. For the majority of my time, you will not find me on any such sites, which has made me vastly unpopular and dorky, but it is worth it for the sake of what God is doing in me.

Maybe your triggers are not the news or social media, but I pray you discover the external sources that trigger your fears and take a break from them. May you go into this part of your journey with excitement. I can say with confidence that when you clear your prayer life of fear-filled pleading, it is magnificent what God can do.

Father God, I pray with excited expectation for my sisters and brothers in you! May you do a mighty work in them as they quiet their prayer lives from fear and open them up fully to you. Lord, I know you have ministries waiting for them, I know you have people in their lives who are dying to be loved on, and I know you desire to be known through their lives! I pray that you will use them to bring glory to you and to bring others to your truth. Father, as fear falls away, I pray that a mighty faith will rise up in them. A faith that causes them to cling daily to your goodness and your power, a faith that could actually move mountains. As they sit with you in prayer, will you allow them to hear your voice in a way they might never have heard before? Lord, I know the powerful change that is at work in them, and I pray that you will come now and solidify it through their times of prayer with you. In the precious name of Jesus, I pray. Amen.

Questions for Reflection

1. How does your prayer life compare with Jesus's prayer life? How is it the same? How is it different?

2. Be honest with God. Is there anything you desire to be taken from your life? Can you trust *him* first with the outcome? Try filling in this blank: "Father, if it is possible, take _____ away. But not my will but yours be done."

3. What are some "greater things" that you could spend time praying for?

4. What is one external thing you could remove from your life to help you focus less on inward fears? How long will you commit to giving it up?

5. Do you find that you spend more time praying for inward things or outward things? Give some examples.

6. What are some examples of things you plead to God about?

7. How can you turn your fear-filled pleas into faith-filled prayers?

8

God's *Promises* of Protection

I had twenty-seven minutes before I needed to be in the car pool line.

Twenty-seven.

What does a wise mother decide to do with such time? Oh, that is easy! Of course, she decides to take her baby and her four-year-old into Lowe's for a "quick" trip. Gotta check off one more thing on the to-do list, so in I go. What could go wrong?

What unfolded next was so embarrassing, so devastating that I told God, *No one can* ever *know about this!* So please, don't tell anyone.

I was in aisle fifteen. My mission was simple: get the wood for the church camp art project and get out. Simple, right? Right.

Aisle fifteen, three minutes into my trip, I am down to twenty-four minutes until car pool line, and then it happened. I had an "accident." Not my baby, not my four-year-old, me. *I* had an accident in aisle fifteen of Lowe's.

The exact details of said "accident" cannot and will not be shared. Some things are meant for Jesus and Jesus alone. But accident it was, and there I stood. Shocked. Amazed. Mortified. *How* did this happen? *Why* did this happen?

Ask me which aisle the bathroom was in? Go ahead, ask me. Yup, aisle one. Aisle *one*! Twenty minutes until car pool line, and off I go. An adult woman with two kids making the longest walk of shame known to man from aisle fifteen to aisle one to try to put a Band-Aid on the disaster that has occurred.

Can I just say, it was a mighty *long* walk. Time slowed, and every step felt like an eternity. I had no choice; all I could think to do was to start claiming the promises of God in my mind.

I interrupt this part of the story to remind you that I am *not* very good at word-for-word Bible memorization. My brain clings to the concepts and the promises, but the details get lost somewhere in the aisle fifteen of my mind. So there I was, blabbering off promises.

Joy comes in the morning; crying cannot last forever and neither will this walk! (Ps. 30:5-ish)

God will not leave me nor forsake me in Lowe's. (Deut. 31:6-ish)

When I walk through the valley of the shadow of death from embarrassment, I will fear no evil. (Ps. 23:4-ish)

When I want to be taken up to heaven—right this very second—I will trust in God's timing. (1 Pet. 5:6-ish)

If a man, who is sinful, knows how to give good gifts to his child, even more so will God give good gifts to his children. Right now I wish that gift would be a pair of pants in aisle one! (Matt. 7:9–12-ish)

I know these sound ridiculous, but at that moment, they were very helpful! I felt so stuck, so trapped, and so un-equipped for the road that lay ahead (even though that road *had* to end in fifteen minutes). It took everything I had not to borrow a shovel from aisle ten and bury myself deep into the ground. I felt foolish, and I did not know what to do.

But God is a God of miracles! I shoved the cart into the handicap bathroom, left the stall door open (because nothing is worth getting your kids stolen over, even utter embarrass-ment), and kept praying for God to take me to heaven—now.

When I got to the car, I prayed, "Dear Jesus, do a miracle! Have something for me to change into in the car!" There it was, in the back seat, one of my long, flowing skirts. Where it came from? Who knows. Like manna from heaven that skirt appeared, and I praised Jesus every second of the way to the car pool line.

I giggled as I thought, *That was just like life.* What an em-barrassing and awful metaphor, but it is so true. When fears come, when life happens, when we don't know how on earth we are going to survive, we do well to speak the promises of God. No matter the road or the fear or the mental battle we are dealing with, the Bible does promise us protection. God does promise to protect us.

No, his protection doesn't always look the way we wish it would. Sometimes we wish that promises of protection would include, for example, the promise that we will *never* under any circumstances have an embarrassing accident in Lowe's when we have only twenty-seven minutes to get to the car pool line. That would be nice, wouldn't it? Or the promise that God will protect us from losing someone we love, financial struggle, or betrayal. In our humanness, we feel robbed that God's promises don't flat-out promise that he will protect us from the things we fear. But when we allow the promises of God to penetrate us to the core, we can take our focus off what we don't know and hone in on what we *do* know.

The first time I led the Breaking the Fear Cycle study at my church, there was a woman in my group who had lost her teenage daughter to suicide. She was a pillar of strength in our group, and her words and prayers always stood out as those of a woman who had gone to the pit of hell and come out still knowing that God is good. I loved her so much. The week we covered this chapter, she looked up at me and with tears in her eyes asked, "Did you compile this list of promises yourself?" I quietly and shyly answered, "Yes, I prayed through each and every one of them." Then she said, "This list is a true treasure, such a gift to me. Thank you."

My prayer is the same for you: that this list of God's promises will be a gift to your soul, one that you fold up and keep in your pocket. A gift you can turn to over and over again when you feel afraid, stuck, or burdened by the pains of this world. God *does* promise to protect us.

God Will Protect You

God's promises of protection over you are vast, and they are *good* promises. It is okay if you can't, don't, won't memorize Scripture. Do whatever works for you to soak in the promises you *need* to remember in times of trouble. It helps me to write them out by hand. My friend pastes them all over her home. My kids write them on index cards. When I was pregnant with Gideon, someone handed me an envelope full of God's promises for me to pull out one at a time. Bookmarks are great too. Do whatever helps you.

It's also okay if only a few of these stand out to you as soothing. God wired us differently and speaks to us as individuals. Cling to the promises you need most in your life, focusing on those that speak deeply to your fears.

May you be blessed, encouraged, and filled with hope as you cling to the goodness of the God who never fails.

Protection from Being Crushed

Many fears come from the terrible thought of falling and never being able to get up again, the lingering fear that something will hit us and take us out forever. This is not so when we have a relationship with the living God! God *will* protect his children from being crushed forever. We may stumble, we may fall, but God will always be there to pick us up.

> But we have this treasure in jars of clay to show that this all-surpassing power is from God and not from us. We are hard pressed on every side, but not crushed; perplexed, but not in despair; persecuted, but not abandoned; struck down, but not destroyed. (2 Cor. 4:7–9)

Protection from Being Uncomforted

It is tempting for us to want to cling to what is seen, yet the very basis of our faith is for us to cling to what is *unseen*. We fear because words, hugs, and nice sayings seem to fall short. They numb the pain for a second, but we know they do not bring full comfort. We wonder, *How can God possibly help me?* Then we fear. But God is the God of the unseen, and he is a God of mighty power. If God can comfort my sweet friend who lost her teenage daughter, if he can comfort me after losing Gideon, if he can comfort missionaries living in dangerous foreign lands for the sake of the gospel, then he *can* and *will* comfort you too. There is *nothing* that can happen to you that God's comfort cannot reach. *Nothing*.

> The LORD is my shepherd, I lack nothing.
>> He makes me lie down in green pastures,
> he leads me beside quiet waters,
>> he refreshes my soul.

> He guides me along the right paths
> > for his name's sake.
> Even though I walk
> > through the darkest valley,
> I will fear no evil,
> > for you are with me;
> your rod and your staff,
> > they comfort me. (Ps. 23:1–4)

Protection from the Evil One

I'm not going to lie; Satan hates seeing us joyful. He hates God, he hates us, and he *loves* our fear. Yes, we live in a fallen world, one full of sickness, tragedy, hatred, and loss. We are not spared from being human. But as children of the King, we are *sealed*. We are God's and God's alone, and Satan has no claim over our lives. Though pain and suffering might still come our way, they are all under God's sovereign rule. Satan wants us badly. When we fear, when we doubt, he may win the battle over us for the day, but he will *never* reign victorious over our lives. God promises us his armor and protection.

> Finally, be strong in the Lord and in his mighty power. Put on the full armor of God, so that you can take your stand against the devil's schemes. For our struggle is not against flesh and blood, but against the rulers, against the authorities, against the powers of this dark world and against the spiritual forces of evil in the heavenly realms. Therefore put on the full armor of God, so that when the day of evil comes, you may be able to stand your ground, and after you have done everything, to

stand. Stand firm then, with the belt of truth buckled around your waist, with the breastplate of righteousness in place, and with your feet fitted with the readiness that comes from the gospel of peace. In addition to all this, take up the shield of faith, with which you can extinguish all the flaming arrows of the evil one. Take the helmet of salvation and the sword of the Spirit, which is the word of God. (Eph. 6:10–17)

Protection from Losing Our Inheritance

If you believe in Jesus, you believe that this life is not all there is. There *has* to be more. These days are all that we can see with our eyes, but they are not all that we can see with our souls. We long for the perfect days of heaven, and our hearts long for the perfect peace that will come in those days. Friends, those days will come! Heaven will be ours! With no pain, fear, tears, or loss, paradise will be ours. Nothing in this life can take that from us. Nothing.

Praise be to the God and Father of our Lord Jesus Christ! In his great mercy he has given us new birth into a living hope through the resurrection of Jesus Christ from the dead, and into an inheritance that can never perish, spoil or fade. This inheritance is kept in heaven for you, who through faith are shielded by God's power until the coming of the salvation that is ready to be revealed in the last time. In all this you greatly rejoice, though now for a little while you may have had to suffer grief in all kinds of trials. These have come so that the proven genuineness of your faith—of greater worth than gold, which perishes even though re-fined by fire—may result in praise, glory and honor when

Jesus Christ is revealed. Though you have not seen him, you love him; and even though you do not see him now, you believe in him and are filled with an inexpressible and glorious joy, for you are receiving the end result of your faith, the salvation of your souls. (1 Pet. 1:3–9)

Protection from Despair

To live in despair is to live in utter loss. When fears come, we get a taste of despair, and it grips us. When we imagine our fears unfolding before us, we see utter loss that is out of our control to prevent, and we become even more fearful. Dear friend, in our own power we *cannot* prevent utter despair. Only God can do that, and he promises that he will! Through one faith-filled step at a time, we can trust that God will give us firm footing to land on. Though a step or two into despair may tempt us to think we are heading there permanently, we most assuredly are not. We may feel despair-filled moments, but God promises not to leave us there. His promise of protection will be there to guide us out of despair.

> The Lord makes firm the steps
>   of the one who delights in him;
> though he may stumble, he will not fall,
>   for the Lord upholds him with his hand.
>   (Ps. 37:23–24)

Protection from Permanent Weeping

Some crying feels like it will last forever. Many mornings, I soaked my pillow all the way through. I wondered if the crying would ever stop, and I clung to the stories of those who went before me. God promises that the joy will return for us. When we cry alongside Jesus, he whispers gently that he loves us and will bring us safely to a place of joy again. The joy might come in little spurts in the middle of the weeping, it might come in one big wave when the weeping is over, it might even take turns with the weeping, but through Christ in us and the hope that comes with him, God promises to protect us from endless, permanent crying.

> LORD my God, I called to you for help,
>   and you healed me.
> You, LORD, brought me up from the realm of the
>   dead;
>   you spared me from going down to the pit.
>
> Sing the praises of the LORD, you his faithful people;
>   praise his holy name.
> For his anger lasts only a moment,
>   but his favor lasts a lifetime;
> weeping may stay for the night,
>   but rejoicing comes in the morning. (Ps. 30:2–5)

Protection from Hopelessness

In all things we have hope. There is *always* hope. We might not always be able to quantify it, measure it, or identify *how* God will solve our hope deficit, but God will find a way. It is his promise, and God does not fail! When we find ourselves full of fearful thoughts, may they be a reminder for us to turn our eyes back to the one and only giver of hope.

Indeed, we felt we had received the sentence of death. But this happened that we might not rely on ourselves but on God, who raises the dead. He has delivered us from such a deadly peril, and he will deliver us again. On him we have set our hope that he will continue to deliver us, as you help us by your prayers. Then many will give thanks on our behalf for the gracious favor granted us in answer to the prayers of many. (2 Cor. 1:9–11)

Protection from Wasted Pain

This is one of my personal favorites. At night when my head hits the pillow and a barrage of fears fill my mind, I stop them dead in their tracks with the promise that God will not waste a minute of pain. My pain is God's pain, and therefore I do not need to fear it. When we love God even more than we love ourselves, this promise can bring us motivation to be strong and courageous. When we cling to this promise of purpose in our lives, we heed not the temptation to allow fear to overtake us. God is good and uses all the moments of our lives to bring us into his likeness.

> Restore our fortunes, LORD,
>   like streams in the Negev.
> Those who sow with tears
>   will reap with songs of joy.
> Those who go out weeping
>   carrying seed to sow,
> will return with songs of joy,
>   carrying sheaves with them. (Ps. 126:4–6)

Protection from Being Alone

God provides. He might show up in presence, he might send the hands and feet of his church here on earth, or he might even send his angels, but he will not leave us alone. Yes, we feel alone sometimes, there is no doubt. When we feel alone, may we implant these verses on our hearts and remember that God will never forsake us. Sometimes the clutter of this life blocks us from finding him or our anxious thoughts keep God at arm's length. Utter these words, and you will find a loving and understanding God waiting to be found.

> Therefore, since we have a great high priest who has ascended into heaven, Jesus the Son of God, let us hold firmly to the faith we profess. For we do not have a high priest who is unable to empathize with our weaknesses, but we have one who has been tempted in every way, just as we are—yet he did not sin. Let us then approach God's throne of grace with confidence, so that we may receive mercy and find grace to help us in our time of need. (Heb. 4:14–16)

Protection from Everlasting Harm

God does promise to protect us from harm. It may not be a promise to spare us from driving off a bridge or having an accident in Lowe's, but it is a promise to keep us from any and all harm that he has not allowed. Not a hair on our heads can be touched without permission from the sovereign God of the universe. We are, quite literally, untouchable.

There is no such thing as arbitrary or random harm that can come to us. Greater still, God sent Christ to protect us from eternal harm. After we die, into his arms we will go, and for all eternity neither death, nor sickness, nor crying, nor pain will ever touch us again.

> I lift up my eyes to the mountains—
>   where does my help come from?
> My help comes from the LORD,
>   the Maker of heaven and earth.
>
> He will not let your foot slip—
>   he who watches over you will not slumber;
> indeed, he who watches over Israel
>   will neither slumber nor sleep.
>
> The LORD watches over you—
>   the LORD is your shade at your right hand;
> the sun will not harm you by day,
>   nor the moon by night.
>
> The LORD will keep you from all harm—
>   he will watch over your life;
> the LORD will watch over your coming and going
>   both now and forevermore. (Ps. 121)

Protection from Death

We rob the cross of its power when we live in fear of death. Christ came to free us from that fear! He suffered, died, and faced hell itself so that we can live in freedom from the fear of death. God knows the fear will still come.

We have thoughts of our spouses dying, our children dying, our friends dying, our family dying, and worst of all, *us* dying and leaving our children to be raised by a husband who still does not know where to find the whisk in our kitchen! There is no shame in the fact that we may experience the fear of death, but may we not be found living in it. May we give credit to the cross of our Savior and embrace the protection we have from everlasting death. Even when we face physical death, we live confident and expectant that eternal life is still to come.

> When the perishable has been clothed with the imperishable, and the mortal with immortality, then the saying that is written will come true: "Death has been swallowed up in victory."
>
> > "Where, O death, is your victory?
> > Where, O death, is your sting?" (1 Cor. 15:54–55)

Protection from Powerlessness

With Christ in us, we are not weak. Why do we fear that we are? We fear as though we are facing a war without defense or weapons; meanwhile, God has given us power that can hardly be fathomed. We cower under our fear, afraid to peek out from under the covers and see the monsters that surround our lives. Instead, may we throw off the covers, pick up our weapons, and take aim at the fears that attack us. God's power is ours for the taking; we need simply to believe it is ours to wield.

For this reason I kneel before the Father, from whom every family in heaven and on earth derives its name. I pray that out of his glorious riches he may strengthen you with power through his Spirit in your inner being, so that Christ may dwell in your hearts through faith. And I pray that you, being rooted and established in love, may have power, together with all the Lord's holy people, to grasp how wide and long and high and deep is the love of Christ, and to know this love that surpasses knowledge—that you may be filled to the measure of all the fullness of God.

Now to him who is able to do immeasurably more than all we ask or imagine, according to his power that is at work within us, to him be glory in the church and in Christ Jesus throughout all generations, for ever and ever! Amen. (Eph. 3:14–21)

Protection from Purposelessness

We feel like aimless wanderers sometimes, don't we? We wonder what on earth we are doing here and how God could *possibly* use someone as small and fearful as us. Friends, if we love Jesus, we have been called to him for a purpose. In him we are protected from being purposeless. Our jobs, schedules, duties, and responsibilities are only a small portion of what defines us. Failure or lackluster in any one of these areas does not translate into purposelessness. Not at all! Instead, we stand firm in the promise that God wants to bring glory to himself *through* our lives.

And we know that in all things God works for the good of those who love him, who have been called according to his purpose. For those God foreknew he also predestined to be conformed to the image of his Son, that he might be the firstborn among many brothers and sisters. And those he predestined, he also called; those he called, he also justified; those he justified, he also glorified. (Rom. 8:28–30)

Protection from Being Unloved

Sometimes we feel so ugly—inside and out. We wonder how anyone could possibly love us. When conflict or betrayal comes, we are tempted to think that we are, in fact, *unlovable.* That surely we have ruined any chance of being loved. It's impossible. Never, not even for one moment of our lives, are we ever unloved. There is nothing that can happen or we can ever do that cannot be redeemed through God's love for us.

> I remember my affliction and my wandering,
>   the bitterness and the gall.
> I well remember them,
>   and my soul is downcast within me.
> Yet this I call to mind
>   and therefore I have hope:
>
> Because of the LORD's great love we are not
>   consumed,
>   for his compassions never fail.
> They are new every morning;
>   great is your faithfulness.

I say to myself, "The LORD is my portion;
  therefore I will wait for him." (Lam. 3:19–24)

His Protection Is Mighty and Strong

As a twenty-year-old brand-new believer trying to figure out how to read the Bible, I decided to read a passage in the Old Testament and a passage in the New Testament every time I sat down to read. I initially determined to read the whole thing front to back, but I got stuck in Leviticus and Deuteronomy and decided that, while I should still read those books, I also needed something a little more applicable. Here I am, all these years later, and I still read a passage from the Old and New Testaments each day. Crazily, during the season of writing this book, the perfect storm has occurred. I am reading Jeremiah in the Old Testament and Revelation in the New.

> His promises of protection are as powerful as he is. Truly, we have nothing to fear.

Since I am in the company of fellow fearers, I can explain to you with full disclosure why this is the "perfect storm." Both of these books are scary to me! They go something like this: death, destruction, death, destruction, torture, plagues, death, and destruction. Then some more death and destruction. The old Maria would have *died* reading this; my thoughts would have been fear, terror, fear, terror, confusion, wonder, fear, and more terror.

But this time, in honor of living the full and true peace-filled life, I put on my untroubled lens and kept reading. This is what I found: God is *amazingly* powerful! He is mighty. I took great joy in reading, knowing that this is the God who is on my side! Jeremiah 32:27 says, "I am the LORD, the God of all mankind. Is anything too hard for me?" Revelation 21:5 says, "He who was seated on the throne said, 'I am making everything new!'"

It is amazing to read two books, side by side, written thousands of years apart, and see that God is the same powerful God yesterday, today, and into eternity. His promises of protection are as powerful as he is. Truly, we have nothing to fear.

> Yes, you have been with me from birth;
>> from my mother's womb you have cared for
>> me.
> No wonder I am always praising you!
> My life is an example to many,
>> because you have been my strength and
>> protection.
> That is why I can never stop praising you;
>> I declare your glory all day long.
>> (Ps. 71:6–8 NLT)

Your Journey

My prayer for you is that you feel your feet planted just a little more firmly on ground that is trustworthy. That God's promises of protection give you something else to stand on when fearful and anxious thoughts come to you. May you fight to keep these truths from God's Word in the forefront of your mind.

Maybe reading and recalling Scripture is new to you, but will you give it a try? As you walk hand in hand with God trying to figure out what helps, I pray *against* shame and guilt and *for* a gleeful, childlike joy. If one method doesn't work for you, try another. Then put into practice what works! Above all else, give God's Word a try on a regular basis. I know it sounds trite, and I hate the burden that comes with the sentence, "Make sure you read God's Word every day." Reading God's Word should come out of the desire of your heart and the *want* and *need* of what he has to tell you—not out of obligation. Obligation does not help to reduce fear. But perseverance does!

As you journey, may God's Word come alive for you. Ask him to show off! Let him know that you need his promises of protection to help you survive. I can say with utter confidence that he *will* show up. As you seek to move away from fear and into God's peace, may your story take you headfirst into the loving, powerful, and trustworthy truth of God's Word.

Father God, I thank you that you do not leave us in this life to journey alone. I thank you that you give us promises that are trustworthy and true, and I pray for the courage to believe in them above all else. Will you help us to bring discipline to our minds so that when fear and turmoil come, we have your Word to stand on instead? Help us to find a way to remember what you say. May you do miracles in our minds as you bring the right Bible passages to us exactly when we need them most. I pray that as my friends come to you for help, you will do for them what you have done for me. Help them to see more clearly than they ever have before, and may their eyes and hearts be open to your promises in a whole new and life-giving way! God, thank you for your power, thank you for your might, thank you for your generosity and love. In all these things, I pray in Jesus's name. Amen.

Questions for Reflection

1. Which one or two of the verses about God's protection touch you the most? Why?
2. Which promises of protection offer you the most security?
3. What is your game plan? What are a few ways you can try to implant God's promises on your heart and in your mind? Will you give them a try this week?
4. What are some specific fears that you have that God promises to protect you from?
5. Will you try praying God's promises of protection? When you don't have words to pray, when you don't have prayers on your lips, will you try reading some of these verses out loud?

9

Taking Jesus Up on His
Offer of Peace

May I tell you a story? It is a story of the greatest peace this life has ever shown me. It is the story of the day that a little piece of heaven came to earth. It is the story of the day Gideon was born.

March 31, a Magical Day

I prayed for a legion of God's angels to be with us that day.

I prayed that God would bring peace and comfort to Gideon in a way that only he can.

I prayed that I could find joy, deep joy, in meeting my son.

I prayed for it all to unfold in God's timing and in God's way.

As I opened my eyes at 4:30 a.m. on March 31, I still did not know when and if God was going to answer these prayers. But as the most intensely precious day of my life continued, every moment revealed his mercy.

The night before, contractions began. I had to breathe through them; the pain grew in intensity. It was five weeks before my due date, and Gideon was coming one way or another. As I stood in the shower, I praised God for the confirmation of his timing that March 31 was the day Gideon was to be born. But then I wondered: Should I change my mind on having the elective C-section?

I had chosen a planned C-section for multiple reasons. I was convinced it was the safer passage for Gideon. We could plan on our children and family being there to meet him when he came. I did not think I could emotionally handle birthing Gideon the same way I had birthed my first three children. Yet amid all these thoughts, my deepest desire was still for God to have *his* way.

When we arrived at the hospital, it seemed the nurses looked at us as if we had fourteen heads! I was thankful for this because I could tell they *knew*, and I understood that they didn't know what to say. I remember that my first stroke of nerves came when I saw my doctor.

I thought, *This is real. This is actually happening. I am going to meet my son. I am going to say good-bye too.*

I told the doctor about my contractions. Then he checked Gideon; he was breeched. Breeched?! He was not breeched two weeks before, and I never noticed a huge turn in him, but sure enough, God confirmed the "how." C-section on

This is the only picture we have as a family with Gideon. Looking at all our faces is a constant reminder to me of the realness of God's peace during those times we need it most. Even our pastor (standing in the background), who watched us cry and grieve and wrestle and suffer, has a sweet smile on his face as he beholds the power of the presence of God.

March 31, as God had always intended. I think my praise started at that moment, and it didn't stop the rest of the day. Pastor Mitch came and prayed over us, and then it was time—time for us to finally meet sweet Gideon.

Even now as I type this, my heart is racing a thousand miles an hour. Oh, what I would have given to stop the clock. To freeze time and never move forward, planted firmly in the few moments I would get to touch my son on this earth. Oh, to freeze time.

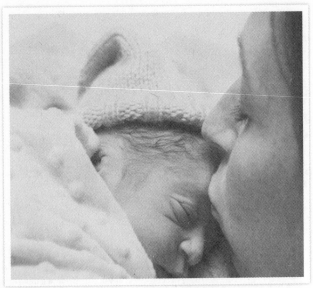

I could have kissed him forever. In my weakest and saddest moments, I weep that my lips will never touch his sweet skin again, but God's joy comes in the morning. Yes, I miss my Gideon every day, but I *will* kiss him again. To that promise I cling. I cherish this picture (and yes, I may kiss the photo sometimes).

Words hardly describe all that came next. No story or utterance does complete justice to the peace that came as the details of Gideon's birthday unfolded before us.

Hearing my husband say, "He's here! He's doing okay. He's not in any pain."

Hearing my sweet son Gideon give out a little cry. A cry! One small sound that only heaven can embrace—the *sweetest* sound of his one little cry—seared into my memory for a lifetime.

The soft, gentle breaths he took while on my chest. His body lay still, his skin on my skin, and his little mouth opened and closed with precious life. If only for a moment, he was mine, I was his mommy.

Looking over as my husband held his son and seeing Gideon's right eye open ever so slightly! I exclaimed out loud with glee, even in the midst of my pain and my crying, "His eye is open! One little eye is open!"

He was pink, he was warm. He was mine to touch, kiss, touch, kiss, and touch and kiss and touch and kiss.

He was always peaceful. *Always* peaceful. From the moment he came until the moment he left, he was peace. He will always be peace to me. As my children touched him and kissed him, as he was baptized, as he was anointed, as he was bathed, as he was dressed, as he was prayed over, as he was sung to, and as he was loved, he was peace. Peace proven true and trustworthy.

Handing him over was the most difficult moment of my life. Touching his touches for the very last time on this earth was a torment that only heaven will heal.

Yet even still. Even still, there was peace.

God's angels were there! I saw them in the sky in a sunrise so magnificent you have to see it to believe it, visual proof for this momma that my prayers had been answered. Our family calls it "the Gideon sky."

God's presence was there, and all our prayers were answered. All of them. The peace that was present in that day left me with this bold and penetrating thought: *Is this what God's peace is? Is this what his promises of peace mean? Then truly, we have nothing to fear.*

I didn't need proof that true peace existed, but God gave it to me anyway. I pray now he will give it to you too. Proof that there is tangible power in the peace that God offers to us. It's a peace so powerful that it overcomes fear; it's a peace that slays fear dead.

A Peaceful Promise

The Bible is littered with peace.

I love BibleGateway.com. It's like Google for the Bible, and I putter around in that search box often. Mostly because, as I told you, I generally remember only parts of Bible verses. Bible Gateway helps me find what I am only partially remembering. But also, I get curious.

I think, *We spend an awful lot of time talking about money in church; I wonder how many times money is mentioned in the Bible?*

Survey says: 113 times.

Okay, well, what about grace? We truly love to talk about grace; how many times is it mentioned in the Bible?

Survey says: 124.

Mercy? 126.

Trust? 170.

Peace? 249.

God *loves* peace—peace of all kinds! He knows us inside and out, and since the beginning of man, since the very first word of Scripture was breathed, he knew how much we would need peace. God offers peace to us often, but we need to make the choice to dive into it to receive its power in our lives.

Imagine you are being chased. Behind you, coming toward you at a fast and intimidating pace, are all your fears. They are merciless, unyielding. They look powerful. Every which way you look, there is nowhere to turn. You come to a pool, with a deep end and a diving board. The pool is called *peace*, and it beckons you to jump in. You walk out onto the diving board, but it doesn't make sense to you. Won't the fears chasing you just follow you in and drown you once and for all? If you stop running, won't they win? But you see no other choice. You've come to the end of yourself.

You jump in.

You look up and see the fears fleeing. They cannot enter peace with you. They are not welcome, and they *cannot* live where peace reigns. Peace envelops and fills you as you float in full submission.

Fear and peace stand in opposition. We cannot experience God's peace if we are dwelling in fear, and, on the other side of the coin, we will not dwell in fear if we are experiencing God's peace. Fear and peace do not live together.

So, then, how do we find peace? How do we take Jesus up on his offer in John 14:27: "Peace I leave with you; my peace I give you. I do not give to you as the world gives.

> Peace envelops and fills you as you float in full submission.

Do not let your hearts be troubled and do not be afraid"? We pray for it at all times, for ourselves and those we love: "May you have peace that transcends understanding!" It is a blessing, and we know deep down that we have a need for it. But in my experience, peace is not something that is poured out over us until we first determine to jump *into* it. Obtaining peace is not a blissful walk in the park; it is a hard-won battle, and peace is the prize.

Let's take a deeper look at one of my favorite passages on peace:

> Rejoice in the Lord always. I will say it again: Rejoice! Let your gentleness be evident to all. The Lord is near. Do not be anxious about anything, but in every situation, by prayer and petition, with thanksgiving, present your requests to God. And the peace of God, which transcends all understanding, will guard your hearts and your minds in Christ Jesus. (Phil. 4:4–7)

What comes before the peace that transcends understanding?

Rejoice in the Lord always.

Rejoice? Really, Lord? But I just found out I lost my job. My child is sick. I had a miscarriage, again. I am surrounded by a million impending fears, and you are asking me to rejoice?

Yes, rejoice always.

Not just sometimes when we feel like it or when we are in a good mood or when circumstances align—rejoice always. This takes some fight.

I think of the stay-at-home mom riddled with fears of not being a "good enough" mom. It is tough enough to endure the mundaneness of her day: pick up this, clean that, discipline this, cry over that. And all the while she is wondering, *Am I worth anything at all?* Rejoice! I will say it again: rejoice. Find it in you, Mom, somehow to focus on rejoicing in any joy you can find.

I think of the man running wildly at work who wonders if he will be able to provide for his family. *It never feels like I am doing enough!* Carrying the weight of the world on his shoulders, pressures mount, and he wonders if he will ever feel content. Rejoice! I will say it again: rejoice. Find it in you, son of the King who created you to do mighty things in him, somehow to focus on rejoicing in any joy you can find.

I think of the woman who wonders, *Will I ever bear a healthy child? Will the pain ever end?* Day in and day out she feels incomplete, lonely, and abandoned. Something inside her prevents her from smiling, from loving, from caring. With tears in my eyes, I say this to you, daughter of the King: rejoice! God has not forgotten you. Though it may seem like it at times, he has a story written for you. It's *your story*. I will say it again: rejoice! Take up your shield of faith and take up the sword of the Spirit. This battle for peace is *yours* to be won!

Let your gentleness be evident to all.

Find opportunities to focus on others. This part of the passage encourages us to go outside ourselves with bold passion and enthusiasm. Become generous with your time and with your words. Minister to those around you who need to be loved on. Tell fear you have no time for it; you are too busy focusing on other people instead. Fear doesn't like it at all when you choose not to focus on *you*.

It was an interesting dynamic; when I was pregnant with Gideon, I found myself comforting others. I would cry and fear in the quiet and lonely times, but I came to appreciate distraction through holding others in their tears. It was a sweet relief that I savored. To this day, I try not to limit God with too many "I can'ts" or "I don't have time for thats." Selflessness is a catalyst to peace, a nonstop trip, and it is a train worth boarding.

May you be a person who never tires in doing good. May you find joy in the opportunity to put yourself and your needs aside for the sake of picking others up. When people utter your name, when your heart comes up in conversations, may your gentleness be evident to all.

The Lord is near.

We sometimes forget that Christ *will* one day return for us. I know I do. In this day and age of media, internet, and knowing all, we get comfortable here. Things seem okay and manageable, and we mostly prefer to manipulate our circumstances rather than remember that the best is yet to come.

Revelation 21 tells us, "He who was seated on the throne said, 'I am making everything new!' Then he said, 'Write this down, for these words are trustworthy and true'" (v. 5).

We are not to walk around in this life as if our days are the end-all and be-all. We have a hope that God will make *all* things new. This is trustworthy and true.

I confessed to you earlier that before Gideon I feared death. Whenever death came up, I would stick my fingers in my ears, close my eyes, and say "Lalalala" like a little girl afraid of monsters in her closet. But there is a way *better* than this.

If you are like me, I encourage you to muster up the courage to face your fear of death. Toss it around in your head, seek what Scripture says, and ask yourself, *What do I really believe about heaven?* Wrestle with God over it until you come to a place of peace. It may take days or even months, but don't stop until you have faced it. Then when fear comes and you remind yourself that the Lord is near, that truth will actually *mean* something to you. You can join me in drifting off into peaceful imagination over what heaven will be like. No pain. No tears. No suffering or death. Sounds wonderful. I look forward to that day with great anticipation!

Do not be anxious about anything, but in every situation, by prayer and petition, with thanksgiving, present your requests to God.

Do not be anxious about anything? Really? Nothing at all? Not many verses are clearer than this one. There is no room for interpretation here; in fact, we can no longer live under the illusion that our anxiety is doing any good work. I know we are often tempted to believe that anxious thoughts might help us. If we ponder them enough, perhaps we will figure out how to stop bad things from happening. Or maybe, if we dwell on them enough, what we fear most won't happen to us. After all, God knows our thoughts, right? Maybe he'll ban that thing from my life because he knows how much anxiety it causes me.

My husband couldn't take it anymore. Expecting his third child, a new role at work, and having to pretend his boss's boss was *not* his father-in-law (when in reality he was) tipped him over the edge. His anxiety came out as a panic attack on a plane ride. What ensued was a two-year battle with anxiety and a newfound fear of flying.

Through counseling and prayer, Dave learned that much of his problem was in his brain. He wasn't able to turn off his anxious thoughts and often found himself defeated. "I guess this is just how I am," he would mutter. But that is not true, and Dave will be the first to tell you that. God does not desire for us to live under the reign of our anxieties. They are not our boss; we are their boss, and we are to *do* something when anxious thoughts appear. Dave fought hard against his anxiety with fervent prayer, relaxation breathing, counseling, and exercise.

Peace is not a call to passivity. Philippians 4:4–7 is not a command to sit back and let God do his work. No! *We* need to do some things to have the peace that transcends understanding:

In everything
By prayer
By petition

With thanksgiving
Present requests
To God

Sit back and do nothing? No! We need to get before a good and holy God, tell him all that we are going through, ask him for what we need, thank him for being a good God who hears our prayers and wants good things for us, and present our anxious thoughts to him. The word choices in this passage of Scripture are so important, each word divinely chosen for us to use and live by.

Your battlefield of prayer might look different from mine or that of the person next to you at church. It doesn't matter; find yours. I cry out in written words in a journal. One of my good friends can only pray out loud and does so *loudly* in her home when it is empty; another friend has a prayer closet. My husband prays in the quiet, some pray on their hands and knees, and others pray while out in nature. God created you uniquely you. May you find your own battlefield and take up your position of prayer with might and power.

> *And the peace of God, which transcends all understanding, will guard your hearts and your minds in Christ Jesus.*

I don't know about you, but my heart and mind could surely use some guarding. This does not mean that fear won't still come at us; what it means is that we have a force field of God's peace surrounding us when it does. Fearful and anxious thoughts might try to take away our peace, but they are diffused. For God's peace, which very much does transcend understanding, is lasting and reliable.

Do you believe this? Can you find it in yourself, in your faith, to *really* believe in that which is unseen?

I have hope—for you and for me. Not because life is perfect once peace comes. Not because I do everything right all the time. But because God is good and has given us guidelines and ideas as to what we can *do* when fear comes. Every day, every moment, may we take up Philippians 4:4–7 as our battle plan, and may we battle with courage and expectancy.

Your Journey

Have you ever read *Jesus Calling: Enjoying Peace in His Presence* by Sarah Young? It is a day-by-day devotional written as if Jesus were speaking directly to us. It is so fun to read what Jesus says to us through Sarah's words, and I am convinced that each day's reading brings exactly what we need at the exact time we need it. It is full of God's words of peace to us.

On the day Gideon was born, I clung especially to the words written for that day. Young spoke of peace unfathomable and how God recognizes that peace is one of our deepest needs. Even on our darkest days, God has peace in store for us.

Would you let these words wash over you for a second? Friend, God wants this deeply for you. Every single day, make the choice to jump back into the deep end of his peace. He wants his lasting gift of peace to be something you live in day in and day out. If it was not so, many of us would be liars. If such peace was not real and attainable, I would have had no words to fill in the pages of this book.

I am not special. Sarah Young is not special. Those who choose to live in God's constant peace are not special. We are desperate! May you be desperate with us.

As you dig through the following reflection questions, I pray that God's miracle of peace will be revealed to you anew. I even pray expectantly for an example this very week of what the surpassing peace of Christ looks like! I have no doubt that God can and will answer that prayer. Will you pray it with me?

Father, I cannot help but praise you for not leaving us alone. That through the presence of your Holy Spirit you have offered us the gift of peace. We are eternally grateful, and I pray now that the enemy of our hearts will stop stealing this truth from us. We believe that your peace is more powerful than our fear and that you have made a way for us to experience your peace—through Christ, through prayer, and through rejoicing, gratefulness, and service. May we bravely accept our call to come to you. My heart wells up. You know that this life will bring pain, and you know that every day we face circumstances and anxious thoughts we cannot control. God, will you help us? Will you come to us now and give us what we need to win the battle? I pray for lasting peace for my sisters and brothers. I pray that you will show them an example of what your trustworthy peace can look like in their days, in their lives. I pray that the scales of doubt will fall from their eyes and they will see, firsthand, a Gideon-sized dose of peace. I thank you for my son. I thank you for the day of his birth. I thank you that through his life I am convinced that nothing can steal your peace from me. I pray the same, Father, for those reading this. May you gift them with your lasting peace. Be with them now in full power and in full peace. In the powerful name of Jesus, this I pray. Amen.

Questions for Reflection

1. What brings you peace?
2. In what ways do you experience peace? Is there a place you go that always feels peaceful? What is it about that place?
3. How do you define peace?
4. When fears come for you, what do you do to replace them with peace?
5. In what areas of your life are you missing peace?
6. Will you give up those areas to God, using the path laid out in Philippians 4:4–7?
7. What is your battle plan of prayer? What are the best ways and when are the best times for you to give over all your anxious thoughts to God in prayer?

10

Living *Differently,* in Confidence

Take my advice: don't write books. Things happen when you write books. I recommend living a quiet and peaceful life, never endeavoring to share your words on paper.

I'm kidding, of course; feel free to write books. Be prepared though: *things* happen when you write them.

There I was, going through my days feeling peaceful and content. I had just finished writing chapter 8, and things seemed to be going smoothly. Sure, distractions came and went, and I constantly found myself praying for the right words, but things were okay.

I was happy. I was content. I was peaceful.

Then came the shake-up. The moment of, "Will you, *can* you live differently, Maria?"

An unplanned pregnancy.

Then an unwanted miscarriage.

Tears hit my keyboard as I sat there deleting all the words I had written *before* the miscarriage occurred, *before* the fear rang true, and once again I found myself sitting in a pile of fear-soaked tears.

What was I to do then? What about all the chapters, the words, the truths I had poured into these pages? When the fear came again, like a tidal wave on a peaceful beach, what then was I to do?

I did the only thing I knew how to do: I dug back into the promises I know to be true. I reached into my fear-fighting tool belt and grabbed at something, *anything*, to get me through the day.

What are my worst fears? I listed them and was honest with God (chap. 1).

First, I am afraid to be pregnant at all.

What if this baby dies too, like Gideon?

What if I have a miscarriage?

What if the baby is stillborn?

What if I can't handle morning sickness this time?

What if I can't finish writing my book?

What if I am too tired?

What if I am too old?

What if my faith fails?

I confessed them all to God, claiming God's power over them and asking God to help me fight the fears once more.

Every morning I woke up and had to re-remind myself of God's promises, gripping white-knuckled to them as if my life depended on it.

>*Maria, focus on today; God's got the future* (chap. 3).
>*Maria, even if these all were to happen, God has never let you down. You know this* (chap. 4).
>*Maria, it's okay to wrestle with God over these circumstances. Go to him often* (chap. 5).

When I had the miscarriage, I was so very hurt and confused. Pain resonated straight out of the Gideon-shaped hole in my heart. I felt out of control and fearful, and I wondered, *Why God?*, and I just wanted to make all the hurt go away again. My daughter was sad, my husband was sad, my family was sad, and sadness and fear usually make uncomfortable companions.

Then I remembered, *Maria, God makes good of your pain. Though you must sit in it for a little while, you know God will not waste your suffering* (chap. 6).

Shoot! Why did I write that chapter? Suffering stinks. Who wants to talk about suffering anyway?

Amid all of my turmoil, I thought about *you*. Through all the fear, confusion, and pain, in the back of my mind was *you*. I prayed for you constantly that when times like these come, you too might muster up the strength to pull out one, even just *one* of God's truths to help you battle your fear. I prayed for you that if and when a time of hurt and suffering comes, you too might find comfort in knowing that God has not forgotten you and that surely he will bring hope to your hurting heart.

I thought about this journey with you, and I wanted to tell you firsthand: *you are not in this alone*. We walk this journey *together*.

Every summer my kids and I make a "bored jar." We find a mason jar and fill it up with activity ideas they can pull out and do on a day they feel bored—aka don't bug Mommy, just pick a slip from the jar and find your own fun! I get a kick out of them because most of the time they go through the entire jar before they find one they like. Or they take a few hours and do every single item in the jar until there are none left. I guess there are no rules when it comes to bored jars.

I like to think of the truths in this book as slips of paper to put into your "peace jar." When fear comes, when your brain cannot turn off, or when life seems to be slamming you in the face, pick a slip of paper out of your peace jar. Maybe you pick through them all before you find the *one* that will help you in that moment or on that day. Maybe one day things are so bad that you need to go through every single one of them. It's okay. There are no rules when it comes to peace jars, but most surely I thank God that I have something to pick from.

Here are the few I've put in my jar to help me live differently:

Take time to list your fears one by one; be honest and tell God. He wants to hear all about them.

Are you going to be a Saul or a David? In your fear, don't act on it, but instead take it to God in prayer and discussion.

Assess your fear: Are you fearing something you worry could happen tomorrow or something you know to be true today? Focus on what you know to be true today.

Even in your worst fears, can you trust God? Yes. Think of the many times he has come through for you in the past. God has never let you down before, and he won't start now.

It's okay to wrestle with God! Take time to go back and forth with him over what you fear. He is faithful to listen and faithful to speak truth. Remember, he is better at control than you are.

Do you believe the Bible to be true? Yes. Then remember that pain and suffering are not things to fear. God is good and uses both for his purposes; therefore, do not be afraid.

Pray big, deep, and wide prayers! Take your eyes off the immediate and the temporal and pray kingdom-sized prayers instead of fear-filled pleas.

God will protect you. Take comfort in his promises of protection; not a thing reaches you that has not passed by God first.

Take a deep breath. Find God's peace—sit in it and soak in it. It is yours, and it is real for the taking. Do whatever you need to do to fight for peace to reign.

We are in this together. We do not move forward feigning perfection or acting like we always have it all together. No. But we do know there is more, and therefore we choose not to live the same. We have a way paved out in Scripture, breathed out in our souls, and printed tangibly in black and white on paper to tap into whenever we need it the most.

When you are lost in the dark, when things happen, when fears come, and when you don't know what to do, may you simply take one step of faith at a time. May you reach back into these truths with courage, and may God's Word wash over you anew every time.

Living in Confidence

With your fear-battling weapons in hand, a new you can arise, one that allows you the freedom to be confident in your new-found peace. After all, once fear is under control, what will you spend your time worrying about? Hopefully, not much. Simply put, God's got it. You *know* this now, and you can be confident in a way you might never have allowed yourself to be.

John Piper, one of my favorite Bible teachers of our time, said:

> I have learned much more about the fight against anxiety. I have learned, for instance, that anxiety is a condition of the heart that gives rise to many other sinful states of mind. Think for a moment how many different sinful actions and

attitudes come from anxiety. Anxiety about finances can give rise to coveting and greed and hoarding and stealing. Anxiety about succeeding at some task can make you irritable and abrupt and surly. Anxiety about relationships can make you withdrawn and indifferent and uncaring about other people. Anxiety about how someone will respond to you can make you cover over the truth and lie about things. So if anxiety could be conquered, a mortal blow would be struck to many other sins.[1]

Dare I say, dare I hope, that we have made a mortal blow? That is my prayer, that together we have given fear and anxiety in our lives a mortal blow. When fear and anxiety go, so goes worry. When worry goes, our outlook on life changes too.

How would life look different if we no longer held on to fears about finances? Living one day at a time, trusting God to provide what we need, when we need it, we are more confident in our jobs, in our homes, in our giving, and in our bank accounts (or lack thereof). We live free from *needing* and *wanting* and stake the claim in our lives that money is not always what's most important. Faithfulness to what we have been given is important. That's it. When we let go of our finance-based fear, we no longer fret about when, where, or *if* to buy a car, change jobs, or allow our children to

> When fear and anxiety go, so goes worry. When worry goes, our outlook on life changes too.

buy yet another Pokémon card to add to their collection. We simply make the best decision we can and then move on. No worry, no fear—just confidence in what we've been given.

How would life look different if we no longer held on to fears about failure? Knowing full well that, in fact, God shows off through our *weakness*, we embrace who we are. We no longer try to change or improve or impress; we simply just be who we are. When we say no to actively fearing our lack of successes or our overabundance of failures, we find contentment and confidence in being who we are. It is so freeing to live this way! Our worth is no longer tied up in what we do; it is firmly tied up in Christ alone. That's it. Everything else falls off our radar as we focus intently on following him in all we do. No worry, no fear—just confidence in who we are.

How would life look different if we no longer held on to fears about relationships? It looks like peace rather than being tempted to overthink every conversation we have or every word that comes out of our mouths. Instead of analyzing every relationship or taking offense in every encounter, we ask ourselves, "Did I have a good heart? Did I intend to speak in love?" Yes, and yes. So we move on in confidence, knowing that it is God who searches our hearts, knows our minds, and defends us. When we do not allow relationships to define us, they become sweet and wonderful additions to our lives. Not necessities, but blessings. Not defining us, but opportunities to shine God's light and love as he loves. When we let go of relationship-based fear, we fight less, we listen more, and we don't email a friend a million times just in case they might be angry about that one thing that came out of our mouth wrong. We know we love well; we claim that truth over our relationships and we live free. No worry, no fear—just confidence in the spouse, parent, child, sibling, and friend God created us to be.

How would life look different if we no longer held on to fears about the future? We live in the present instead. We live more fully, more freely, and more joyfully in whatever *now* brings. We take captive thoughts that bind us to a tomorrow we cannot control and instead focus on the today we have to live. Letting go of our fears about the future helps us enjoy the moment. We savor our tasks big and small and let go of the minor stresses of life. We are free to be less controlling, less manipulative, and less opinionated. It helps us not to immediately jump to the worst-case scenario over the lump we found on our child. Tomorrow we may take them to the doctor if necessary, but *for today* we have them to love and to hold. It helps us not to be afraid when a loved one gets sick or receives a scary diagnosis because *for today* they are still here. It helps us not to imagine our spouses in car wrecks, affairs, or joblessness because *for today* that is not what we know to be true. It helps us not to focus on whether a miscarriage is imminent or whether God will allow us to have a child at all, for we have no control over either. We stop imagining the worst and simply live. We dream gently and trust fully. No fear, no worry—just confidence in the *today* that God has given us to live.

In all of these things we will never be perfect. We will still fail, we will still fear, and we will still worry. But we will not *remain* there like we used to! What used to be weeks, months, or years of intense fretting will now become minutes, hours, or days. When we are slammed with all the fear that used to overtake us, we will brace ourselves and turn boldly back to the truths we have learned. We will still hurt, still have pain, and still mourn loss, but we will stand strong with *hope* and find comfort in *peace*. We will remember what God has promised us and know how to get there.

> Peace I leave with you; my peace I give you. I do not give to you as the world gives. Do not let your hearts be troubled and do not be afraid. (John 14:27)

Your Journey

We are almost to the end of the road. We will part soon, and my heart is saddened for our journey to come to an end! But for you this is only the beginning. The practice field has been intense. You have worked hard and journeyed bravely, allowing your mind and spirit to enter into places you have never gone before. You have dug deeply into God's Word, and I am expectant that the Holy Spirit moved in you as you read.

I wonder what your story looks like now. I wonder if the "you" of chapter 1 thinks the same as the "you" of chapter 10. The reflection questions below are meant to help you identify areas where you have grown and to celebrate them.

At this point in the process, I pray that you will come up with your own version of a battle plan. I am a pull-a-piece-of-paper-from-the-jar-type person. Doing so helps me to go one by one through the truths we learned together in order to combat fear in my life. Your plan, however, might look different, and that is okay. Maybe you need to remember only one or two points in times of need, such as "Stay firmly in whatever *today* holds, no future thinking" or "Bring your fears to God *before* acting on them." Maybe you love to write, and you write a letter to yourself advising the fearer in you what to do in case of an emergency. Whatever you do, be you and be bold! Hold tightly to what has impressed you most through the reading of this book.

As I pray for you now, I cannot help but be excited for you. God honors the hearts of his children who seek him. The very fact that you made it to these last chapters shows that you are *in it* for whatever God has for you. You are faithful, you are strong, you are brave, and God will be glorified because of your trust in him. Thank you for allowing me the honor and giving me the joy of coming alongside you. Doing so has blessed my life more than you will ever know.

Father, you are good. You don't leave us when we need you, you hear the cries of our hearts, and you know well what is good for us. Thank you for bringing us this far! Will you help us know how to keep these truths at the forefront of our minds? Will you show us how to access your fear-fighting truths in times when the floodgates open? Will you guide us hand in hand down a path that will be the most help to us when we need it? Lord, I pray that you will be with my sisters and brothers now. I pray that you will reveal to them a battle plan that most fits who you created them to be. Show them the truths that you want implanted on their hearts and minds. May we never forget! Though we stumble and fall, we are never crushed, and we praise you! Come now, Holy Spirit, and bring to conclusion the work you began in us in chapter 1. We are yours, we trust you, and we thank you. In the precious name of Jesus, I pray. Amen.

Questions for Reflection

1. Time to make a new list! What are your greatest fears?

2. Compare today's list with the list you compiled in chapter 1. How are they different?

3. Which chapters stood out the most to you? Why?

4. If you could tattoo one fear-fighting truth on your forehead (figuratively speaking), what would it be?

5. What is your battle plan? What are some tangible ways you can be reminded how to fight fear when it comes?

6. What are some visual reminders you can place in your life, in your home, or in your workplace?

7. Will you take a minute to allow God to breathe Psalm 23 over your life and your days? What most stands out to you about his promises in these verses?

The LORD is my shepherd, I lack nothing.
    He makes me lie down in green pastures,
he leads me beside quiet waters,
    he refreshes my soul.
He guides me along the right paths
    for his name's sake.
Even though I walk
    through the darkest valley,
I will fear no evil,
    for you are with me;
your rod and your staff,
    they comfort me.

You prepare a table before me
    in the presence of my enemies.
You anoint my head with oil;
    my cup overflows.
Surely your goodness and love will follow me
    all the days of my life,
and I will dwell in the house of the LORD
    forever.

11

The *Story* of You

I have not "arrived."

You have not "arrived."

I believe that is, in fact, why Jesus came to die for us. There is no "arriving" in life; try as we might, we will never be perfect on this side of heaven. Our full and flawless arrival awaits us in eternity and not a minute sooner.

Yet, while we wander through this life together, may we be encouraged by the fact that God is writing a story in us, and he has beautiful things to say. The story of *you* is one of the greatest stories ever written. It has joy and tears, faith and fear, successes and failures, and it is *just right*. God loves your story; I pray that you will grow to love it too.

In this book, I have shared with you *my* story, not only the story that God has been weaving in me but also how his redemption created a whole new me. Thank you for allowing me to share it with you.

I would like to share the stories of others who have walked this road with us through the Breaking the Fear Cycle class I taught at church. With courage *and* fear, they faithfully pursued what God would have for them. May you be encouraged by the knowledge that none of us journey alone. Though our stories are perfectly unique, our struggles are not, and together we can see that living in real peace is possible.

God is writing a story in us, and he has beautiful things to say.

As you read these stories, I pray that you will consider these questions: What is my story? What is God doing in me? I promise you, people want and *need* to hear what God is doing in your life. God wants to use *you* to bring glory and honor and praise to his name for all the mighty work he is doing in you.

Meet my friends.

Name: Ashley W.

Age: 38

Greatest fear: Not being in control.

Favorite truth: God is so much better at being in control than I am.

By the time I reached my thirties, I was carrying around a lot of fear. My journey to that point in life was not fraught with a big life event or even a series of smaller ones that would have resulted in my becoming so fearful. I would not have considered myself a fearful person in my younger years, and when looking at my life, you would probably think, *What in the world would she have to be fearful of?* That's what was so troubling about it. Fear was something that ever so slyly crept quietly into my heart over time.

Even as a lifelong Christian, I had unknowingly opened my heart to many worldly lies. I had come to believe (even if only subconsciously) that *I* was responsible for all that was good in my life. *I* had worked hard to get to where I was. If *I* continued to work hard and make all the right decisions, then *I* could keep bad things at bay and control what would happen in my life. These lies, along with others, such as "I am not good enough," "I am not smart enough," "That went wrong because I was not paying enough attention," planted the seeds of fear in my heart. As time went on, the *less* in control of a situation I was, the *more* the fear bubbled up.

In my midthirties, I had become mother to two sweet children, and I should have been enjoying all motherhood has to offer. But below the surface, I found myself always worrying about being a good mom and fearful of parenting in so many ways. I felt like I had tried to control and then failed over and over and over again. I remember feeling trapped sometimes, unwilling to make a move in any direction because I was so unsure about whether the next step would be a success or a failure. I think I started trying to keep my world as small as possible so that I could control all of it. But even so, things felt more and more out of control. My worries in regard to being a good mom spilled over into other areas of life as well. I second-guessed myself in everything, and fear was beginning to rob me and my family of all the joy life has to offer.

By the grace of God, one semester our church offered Breaking the Fear Cycle as a study. God's timing is always perfect, and he spoke clearly to my heart, "You are to be a part of this study." Seriously, my conviction was so strong that it really was more of a command than a gentle prodding! During those ten weeks, as I began to make the choice to open my heart to God's promises and truths in regard to fear, God began to do a big work in me.

There are so many things I could say about what God has taught me since walking into that first class. But most important is that through the steps he taught Maria, that she in turn shared with us, I now know that I do not have to be chained in this world to fear. Fear will come, but now I have the God-given promises and truths I need to keep it from controlling my life. All that time, I had been working hard to control everything when, in reality, fear was controlling me! And now I know it doesn't have to be that way and wasn't meant to be that way!

There have been so many times I have called upon the biblical truths I learned in those ten weeks, and I fully expect that I'll continue to do so. The truth is, I think I will always struggle with giving up control. But our gracious God walks beside me and reminds me to let go and let him have it.

God also taught me during that time that this life and all that comes with it is a journey, one that I now appreciate rather than fear. It's a journey in which I am called to be an active participant, but not the orchestrator. For me, freedom and true peace reside in the promise that God is truly good and sovereign over all.

———————————

Name: Julia B.

Age: 36

Greatest fear: That something terrible will happen to me or my children, and I will never be able to recover from it.

Favorite truth: God uses pain for his purpose.

I am not the type of person who fears something *before* it happens, but I am the type of person who fears something *after* good things have occurred. Fear generally comes upon me after a really great day or a fun adventure with my family. I think, *What if* this *or* that *had happened? What if I hadn't been watching?* When those kinds of thoughts hit me, the most crippling fear comes over me and I think, *How would I ever be able to move on if something bad* did *happen?* The chapter that most addressed this fear for me was chapter 6: "Believing in the Bible's View of Suffering." In this lesson, the Bible verse from James 1 really stood out to me: "Blessed is the one who perseveres under trial because, having stood the test, that person will receive the crown of life that the Lord has promised to those who love him" (v. 12). I truly believe that how we think and feel will change outcomes.

In reflecting on this belief and the verse in James, I wrote this in my journal:

> Give up the fear that I will not make it through the suffering. Keep your mind focused on God, his grace, his blessings, and you will survive it all. The end result will be worth it.

I know that does not mean that when I go through suffering in my life, it will be easy; God tells us in the Bible that it is not always going to be easy. But I understand now that if I truly believe in who God says he is, then I have no reason to fear suffering.

Name: Kari M.

Age: 40

Greatest fear: Not being able to know the future for my children, my marriage, my life.

Favorite truth: God holds the future in his hands, fights my battles, and will always be with me.

I was in the middle of separating from my husband. The worst had come, and I found myself in a situation I did not want to be in. I was afraid and questioning myself. *Do I really trust God is taking care of me and my kids? If I do believe that, then why am I constantly trying to control everything?* The study Breaking the Fear Cycle came during a time when I needed it most. I learned that I fear because I cannot control, but I try to control because I fear. I fear because I can't control what happens to my family and my children. I fought for my marriage and family, and finally there was nothing left I could do but lay them on God's altar, asking him and him alone to take care of them.

I left my husband, my dream home (I had moved cross-country less than two years earlier), my new friends, my belongings, my lifestyle, and my dreams—and fears hit me on a daily basis. To survive I *had* to learn to daily trust God. I found myself on a scary, unknown journey but with a known and trusted God. He gave me ways to find faith. I learned that God *is* in control; I just don't always accept that fact because I don't see it. Living in faith requires me to trust God to look after me even when I have an unknown future and child custody issues pending. In the middle of my tears, I had to *choose* to let God write the script of my life.

Every day I have to fight fears of my next steps. How am I going to make it through moving away to get help, which means taking the kids away from their new friends, new home, and their dad? How am I going to raise the kids on my own as a single mom? How am I going to survive the rejection and betrayal of the man I married, who was my best friend? Will I be reconciled or divorced? How am I going to face my family and friends and tell them what is happening? How am I going to make it through sitting in a courtroom with my future in the balance? Will I be able to trust that truth will prevail? Will the kids be okay without me when they're with their dad? How can I help my kids through their hurt and help heal their pain? These and many other fears flooded my mind over and over again, and I realized that I was future telling and leaving God completely out of it all. God began to challenge me. *Am I enough? Not only for you but also for your kids? Do you trust me with them?* It was tough to trust God with my future and family, but the message kept ringing true in my heart that "he would fight my battles and I only needed to be still." My efforts and energy failed in comparison to his ability. Now when the pain comes and it hurts to think of the future, I remember that God will be there to help me. He has and will continue to fight for me. After all, hasn't God always provided me with enough? In every situation, yes, he has!

There is no doubt that this new journey I find myself on is hard, but with my God it is not without hope. God has gone before me, and I find peace, even in the midst of fear, in remembering that he will always be with me. Fear forgets the Father, but faith finds him! Even when lies and manipulation seem to rule, God is faithful. No, I am not the answer for my children's safety and well-being. It is not *my job* to control every situation I find myself in. My kids are God's kids first, and he does a better job than I do. Psalm 27:13 says, "I remain confident of this: I will see the goodness of the LORD"—one day at a time, one foot in front of the other, focused on a future that includes him, and freed to live today because he's got this, and I don't have to try to control it anymore. Be at rest once more, O my soul, for the Lord has been and will be present with me.

Name: Dave Furlough

Age: 35

Greatest fear: Not being able to handle what life throws
   at me, including personal physical discomfort and
   failing at balancing and excelling in work, parenting,
   marriage, relationships, and ministry.

Favorite truth: "The weapons we fight with are not the
   weapons of the world. On the contrary, they have
   divine power to demolish strongholds. We demolish
   arguments and every pretension that sets itself up
   against the knowledge of God, and we take captive
   every thought to make it obedient to Christ"
   (2 Cor. 10:4–5).

Life was good. I had a great job, three wonderful kids,
and an awesome wife. We were settling in at an amazing new
church, and I was taking classes to earn my master's degree.
But right about the time I celebrated my thirtieth birthday,
things started to change. I began to feel overwhelmed with
life: my job responsibilities were getting harder, and I was
balancing working from home, being a dad of three young
kids, and taking classes for my advanced degree. Then my
travel schedule at work began to pick up. By nature, I am an
introvert who gets energized when I can get away from life
either alone or with just my wife, so traveling was stretching
me. While on a plane ride home from a work meeting in
Dallas, I had my first panic attack. I started to feel dizzy and

nauseous, and immediately my mind starting racing. Fearful thoughts started coming: *I can't get sick here; there is nowhere for me to go*. My body and mind were freaking out.

Over the next few months, I experienced a few more of these types of episodes. What ensued from there was a whole lot of fear. What if this happens again? How can I go out in public? What if I need to go to a mental hospital? What's wrong with me?! Am I this weak? I was in a desperate place. I tried various types of medications, some leading to suicidal thoughts, and none really helped. For about a year I struggled with finding answers. If this truly is "all in my head," why can't I just pull it together? And why am I having such a hard time leaning on God? Why isn't he giving me clear answers when I need them? The fear was so crippling that I avoided many situations and became depressed at my choice to retreat. I prayed a lot for God to heal me, and then two major things happened. (1) I met with a Christian psychologist several times and talked through my anxiety with him. He taught me much about myself and always pointed me back to reliance upon God. He reminded me to take captive my thoughts, keep my eyes on things unseen, not to give in to lies, and most importantly, that I don't have to be in control. God is in control, and he knows my every step. (2) Shortly after meeting with him, my wife and I walked through the birth and loss of Gideon.

Gideon taught me so much. There was a time when I said, "There is no way I can stand at his graveside, see an infant casket, and be able to handle it." After our journey from fear to faith during Maria's pregnancy with Gideon, I spoke about peace as we laid him to rest at the very grave site I thought I could never stand beside. The two chapters called "You Do Have a Choice" and "Fear and Future Telling" most helped me. Naming my fears and realizing that I have specific choices in how to deal with them were freeing. Steering away from projecting negative thoughts into the future based on those fears has been life changing. Through Gideon, God taught me what true peace looks like and how that can apply to any situation in life. I now look at fear and anxiety as natural feelings that, when put in their place, are very small in the scheme of life. If I can see my son both be born and go to heaven in a matter of minutes, then I can certainly face anxiety and fear head-on, fighting with the weapons God gives. Fear and anxiety still come and go in my life, but I have learned to rest in God's arms through it all. We truly can have victory (with Christ) over fear. I cannot imagine walking this life without him.

It is so precious for me to close with Dave's words. I might be the one writing about our journey, but we traveled together from a fear-filled life to a peace-filled life. And how different our fears were! But God? *He* is the same, and he ministers to us perfectly with a truth that transcends different fears, circumstances, or personality types.

As we close, I pray these words over you, spoken from God's heart to yours.

My child, my ways are not your ways. I don't always work according to facts, time, or reason. My plan unfolds over time, and I am calling you, my beloved, to trust in my plan. I love you deeply! I do not desire to punish you or haphazardly make things difficult for you. There is wisdom and purpose behind everything I do. Come to me when you feel afraid, come to me when you wonder, come to me when you feel sad or unsure. I am here for you always; I do not desire that you wander alone. I have plans for you. Your story will take years to unfold. Remember, your concept of time is not my concept of time. Focus on today and eternity. The rest is up to me. It is simple for me to make your life fit wonderfully together. My gift to you is my sovereignty over you. I am asking you to let go of trying to figure it all out. Your life is a beautiful mystery. I have given you the gift of hindsight instead. In looking back, you can see the glory of my ways. You can see the beautiful tapestry I am making of your life. When you are tempted to despair, look back at what I have already done and see that I am good! Look behind you and see that I will never leave you! Look behind you and see how much I love you! Look behind you and see all the times I have carried you and taken care of you. I will always be with you. Always. My sweet child, rest now from your fears. Stay calm. Trust me. I have you.

Your Story

Will you add your story to this chapter? Would you bless the world with the telling of your story and what God has done in and for you?

The wonderful thing about God's stories is that they are never meant for only one person to enjoy. The light of his story in our lives is one that needs to shine and be shared. May you be blessed as you realize that you now can help others in their fears. May you love God's story in you so much that you have to share it. Maybe it is with a spouse, a friend, a family member, or a child, but may you find the opportunity to tell someone!

These last moments are meant for you to write your story. If you'd like to, in a journal, write your name, age, greatest fear, and favorite truth, along with your story and your prayer.

May you be blessed as each and every day God pours peace over your troubled heart anew.

Leader's Guide

Introduction

It's time, isn't it? It is time to stop living in fear! May you be blessed as you lead others to live freely in the peace about which the Bible speaks so often. I believe you know it is time because you were brave enough to choose to lead others through this study.

This book is a call to an interactive journey between you, your group, and your heavenly Father, who wants more for you than to live shackled in fear. It is a battle plan, a call to prayer, and an opportunity for you to fight for the peace that is truly yours to live in.

I want you to know I am walking with you. I have been praying for you on this journey, and I believe God has amazing things in store for you and your group!

I want to take a minute to prep you for what lies ahead.

Prayer and leaning into the power and guidance of the Holy Spirit are the two most important characteristics of this journey. Reliance upon God in prayer and a listening heart are far more important than eloquent stories, class preparation, or homework. As you lead this group, plan to meet for about two hours and consider including the following elements in each session:

- Provide a brief time at the beginning of each class for people to share about their most recent run-ins with fear and how they handled them.
- Open in prayer, always.
- Read together the Bible passages in each chapter and present some or all of the questions at the end of each chapter; be comfortable waiting a minute or two in silence for people to process and share.
- Offer a portion of class time when people can sit, listen, and journal alone with God.

This is the beginning of the journey, both for you and for the people in your group. It is no small thing that God has called you to, but take a deep breath! This is God's show to run! One of the most important things you can do as the leader is to be *real*. Use this content as a guide and a help, not a script. Read through each week's chapter and pray over it. Let the Lord guide you as you prepare and give over to him exactly what you will or will not cover. Be blessed and know that every word has been prayed over in abundance!

Welcome the Group

Begin the first session by welcoming your group. You may wish to use the following as a guide: "Walking this journey together is an exciting thing. Cover your study time in prayer and move forward with full confidence that God has something very special in store for you!

"Your time here will be more than a Bible study; it will be a journey and an opportunity for God to move powerfully. May his Word and his promises jump into your heart, and may you tangibly see what God does when you allow him to move in you.

"Before we get into this week's chapter, let's go over a few details about the study so you have an idea of what to expect."

Practice Makes Perfect

The format of this book study is designed to give you and the group an opportunity to put into practice some spiritual disciplines that will help in the journey from fear to faith. If you and others in the group are familiar with these disciplines and they have been a part of your faith journey, keep going! For those who are not familiar with these disciplines, encourage them to prayerfully push past the discomfort and unfamiliarity and to give them a try. Ridding your heart of fear, living in faith, relying on God's Word, and welcoming in God's Holy Spirit are part of a process and a path you will all embark on together!

Journals

Each member of the group will need a journal and will need to be ready and willing to use it. This journal is going to be an important part of every single session, and as you journey together I offer this challenge: during the course of this book study, use the journal for keeping track of prayers (prayers asked and answered) and as your record of all God does in your heart during this time.

For those who have not used journals before, provide an example or two during each session of how to use the journaling time. A great way to start is by writing out prayers word for word, like a letter to God.

Journals will be *private* unless someone chooses to share.

Active Listening

During this journey, you and your group are going to practice listening and recording what you hear God saying to you. Sometimes people are hesitant to do this. They say, "No, that couldn't really have been God; it must have been the voices in my head." And then they move on with their day.

For you and the group? Instruct them as follows: "During this time, first write down what you hear God speaking and then later test it. Those little promptings that are so faint they are easy to ignore—write them down. Those nudges that you get but don't trust yourself enough to determine whether they are from God—write them down. Then in prayer specifically ask God to reveal to you what he meant. Balance them with Scripture; if something contradicts even one word of the Bible, it was not God speaking to you. You can also test the promptings by sharing them with a trusted, Christ-following friend."

Encourage the group to go through the process of actively listening to what they hear God saying and writing it down. Perhaps offer an example of active listening prayer time in your own life.

Take time each session to practice actively listening to God. It is *that* important. The only way to begin to fight fear in our lives is to listen, hear, and trust the quiet voice of God over the loud yelling of our fears.

God does speak to us. When we hear and respond, it is a powerful thing.

Day-to-Day Trust

One of the things you and your group are going to study in this class is how to live *one day at a time*, living moment to moment instead of striving to plan and control. To practice this in a small way, encourage the group not to jump ahead in the book, maybe not even read the table of contents! Dive into one chapter at a time, letting God work fully in and through you on that topic before moving on to the next. Basically: no peeking!

Confidential

When people share, acknowledge as a group that all is confidential, that no one will share with anyone outside the group unless given permission to do so.

God Meets Us Differently

As part of the active listening and sharing with one another, remember that God meets us all differently. As many people as there are in the group, God has just as many ways to bring us on the journey from fear to faith.

Even as different as we are, however, we need each other so that we may see:

1. The journey is possible. Our personal stories are living and breathing testimonies to the fact that we can live without fear.
2. We are not alone.

As the leader, take an opportunity to share your own fear-to-faith journey. Be vulnerable and brave! What were the deepest fears you faced? How were they controlling your life? You can do this!

Your Plan of Action

Here is your battle plan—a recommended schedule. Feel free to abridge or edit the schedule to best meet the needs of your group.

15 minutes—Catch up on life! How was your week? Did God do anything amazing? Did you face any huge fears you weren't expecting?

30 minutes—As a group, read through the Bible passages included in the chapter. What verses stood out to you? Did anything confuse you or intrigue you? What was your takeaway from these passages? Pick out points from the chapter to discuss, and ask group members to do the same.

30 minutes—Choose one or two of the "Questions for Reflection" at the end of the chapter and discuss them together as a group.

30 minutes—Journal together. Choose one or two questions from the end of the chapter and have some alone time with God to journal answers.

15 minutes—Pray over one another! Share prayer needs, lay hands on one another, and lift one another up in encouragement and prayer!

Appendix

In Case of an Emergency: *Bible Verses to Post around Your Life*

Be strong and courageous. Do not be afraid or terrified because of them, for the LORD your God goes with you; he will never leave you nor forsake you. (Deut. 31:6)

> In peace I will lie down and sleep,
>   for you alone, LORD,
>   make me dwell in safety. (Ps. 4:8)

> I love you, LORD, my strength.
> The LORD is my rock, my fortress and my
>   deliverer;
>   my God is my rock, in whom I take refuge.
>   (Ps. 18:1–2)

Wait for the LORD;
    be strong and take heart
    and wait for the LORD. (Ps. 27:14)

The LORD gives strength to his people;
    the LORD blesses his people with peace.
        (Ps. 29:11)

God is our refuge and strength,
    an ever-present help in trouble.
Therefore we will not fear, though the earth give
    way
    and the mountains fall into the heart of the sea.
        (Ps. 46:1–2)

When I am afraid, I put my trust in you.
    In God, whose word I praise—
in God I trust and am not afraid.
    What can mere mortals do to me? (Ps. 56:3–4)

Truly my soul finds rest in God;
    my salvation comes from him. (Ps. 62:1)

The LORD will watch over your coming and going
    both now and forevermore. (Ps. 121:8)

Have no fear of sudden disaster
    or of the ruin that overtakes the wicked,
for the LORD will be at your side
    and will keep your foot from being snared.
        (Prov. 3:25–26)

A heart at peace gives life to the body.
    (Prov. 14:30)

The fear of the LORD leads to life;
    then one rests content, untouched by trouble.
        (Prov. 19:23)

Jesus looked at them and said, "With man this is impossible, but with God all things are possible." (Matt. 19:26)

And surely I am with you always, to the very end of the age. (Matt. 28:20)

I have told you these things, so that in me you may have peace. In this world you will have trouble. But take heart! I have overcome the world. (John 16:33)

May the God of hope fill you with all joy and peace as you trust in him, so that you may overflow with hope by the power of the Holy Spirit. (Rom. 15:13)

And the God of all grace, who called you to his eternal glory in Christ, after you have suffered a little while, will himself restore you and make you strong, firm and steadfast. (1 Pet. 5:10)

Acknowledgments

First and foremost, I want to thank my heavenly Father. He has never given up on me, he has entrusted to me far more than I deserve, and he is good. He always listens, he always teaches, and I love him so.

Dave, I can say with confidence that I have made it to this point in my writing life because of you. You have *always* encouraged me and believed far more in me than I have ever believed in myself. You are my biggest cheerleader and the best husband-editor this world has ever known. You are so good to me. When I was thirteen years old, I prayed a quiet prayer to God about the husband I would like to marry someday. He answered my prayer and then some when he blessed me with you. I love you.

To my Faith, my sweet girl. You have stolen my heart since the day you were born, and I thank God every day for gifting me with you. Thank you for teaching me so much. Thank you for challenging me and believing in me. Thank you for getting excited whenever I talk to you about my writing. Mommy loves you more, impossible!

To my David. You were the first to teach me what it means to love a son. You are so smart and fun, and I love all the many ways you are like both Mommy and Daddy. Your compassionate heart is the sweetest. Thank you for always being my helper and peacemaker. You are all that Mommy could dream of in an oldest son. Mommy loves you more, impossible!

To my Aaron. You have been by my side since the very beginning. You are a devoted and true companion, and I can always count on you for someone to just be with me. Thank you for being so handy around the house. You were always there to be my assistant at home and with Sammy whenever I needed it most. Mommy loves you more, impossible!

To my Gideon. You changed me. From the inside out, God used you to make me new, and I will be forever grateful to you for that. In so many ways, this book is in honor of you. With every kick in my belly and every kiss on your cheek, I fell deeply in love with you. I miss you so much, and I dream of the day I get to hold you again. Mommy loves you more, impossible!

To my Sammy. I don't think anything has felt sweeter in my arms than those chunky little legs of yours. You brought so much joy to this family and to my heart, and you helped my mommy heart heal. Thank you for your smiles, your "guh guy," and your kisses. Thank you for letting me write and be your mommy at the same time. Mommy loves you more, impossible!

To Mom and Dad. You have always encouraged me to keep going and told me that I could do anything I put my mind to. Thank you for being there for me through the ups and downs. You have been ever faithful and loving to me, and I will be forever grateful for you.

Thank you to my family. Thank you to Nick for all our car conversations and for keeping me grounded. Did you even know I was writing a book?

Thank you to the sisters I've always wanted. Bre, Nancy, Jenny, and Rachel, thank you for teaching me about fashion so I don't look ridiculous in my meetings, thank you for showing me how nice it is to have a sister to pick up the phone to call when I need a chat, and thank you for all the laughter.

To the rest of the DeBeauvernets, Bolingers, Furloughs, and Goddards, and Debbie and Dave. You have been there for our family through thick and thin, and your love and support mean the world to us.

Thank you to all our New York, New Jersey, and Florida family, especially Grandma, Grandpa, Nana, and Popie. You have loved on me and believed in me since day one. Thank you.

Thank you so much, Andrea, for believing in my work and for giving me a chance. I will be forever grateful!

To the rest of the Revell team. Every single moment working with you has been a joy. You are an amazing group of people, and I am honored to know you.

I have been blessed with friends beyond compare. Thank you, Carrie, Cammie, Lindsey, Greta, Ashley, Julia, Kim,

Marissa, and Karrie, for always having faith in me, for listening to all my crazy venting, and for encouraging me to keep going.

Thank you, Myquillyn and Emily, for being my mentors in writing and for teaching me all that I know. And thank you for creating the awesomeness that is Hope*Writers.

Thank you, Mitch, for counseling us, crying with us, pastoring us, and praying with us. God used you in miraculous ways to shepherd our family here.

Thank you, Lindsay. Your creative presence is more of a blessing to me than you might ever fully know. Thank you for making things beautiful.

To our entire Lake Forest Church community. Thank you for walking us through the hardest time in our lives, and thank you for allowing me to teach my message to you first. You are truly our family.

To all of my endorsers. Receiving support from you encouraged me and bolstered me greatly. Thank you!

To my amazing Hope*Writer friends, especially my Hope Circle. Thank you for living in these crazy waters with me. It is a joy writing and doing life with you.

Notes

Chapter 6 Believing in the Bible's View of Suffering

1. Nancy Guthrie, ed., *Be Still, My Soul: Embracing God's Purpose and Provision in Suffering* (Wheaton: Crossway, 2010), 26.

Chapter 7 Praying Faith-Filled Prayers, Not Fear-Filled Pleas

1. Emily Freeman, *Simply Tuesday: Small-Moment Living in a Fast-Moving World* (Grand Rapids: Revell, 2015), 178.

2. Chip Ingram, *The Invisible War: What Every Believer Needs to Know about Satan, Demons, and Spiritual Warfare* (Grand Rapids: Baker Books, 2007), 187.

Chapter 10 Living Differently, in Confidence

1. John Piper, *Future Grace: The Purifying Power of the Promises of God* (Colorado Springs: Multnomah Books, 2016), 51.

Maria Furlough is a wife, a mother of five (four on earth and one in heaven), and the head of women's ministry at Lake Forest Church in Huntersville, North Carolina. She has been writing and teaching Bible studies for fourteen years and currently writes on the blog *True Worth* at www.mytrueworth.org. Her favorite thing to do is lead others to the hope and peace that she has found in Christ. The occasional flash mob is not so bad either.

Connect with
Maria!

Learn more about Maria and her
speaking engagements, and read her blog at

MariaFurlough.com

#breakthefear

f @Maria.Furlough

⊙ @MariaFurlough

✉ MariaFurloughAuthor@gmail.com

Show Your Daughter the Way to Confidence

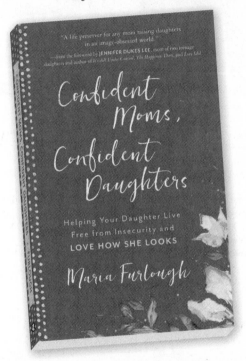

With deep compassion, Maria Furlough delves into the root causes of our insecurity, offers biblical guidance for seeing ourselves as God sees us, and shows how to model our newfound confidence to our impressionable daughters. What we say to our daughters lasts a moment. What we show our daughters lasts a lifetime.

LET'S
TALK
ABOUT
BOOKS

- Share or mention the book on your social media platforms.
  Use the hashtag **#breakthefear**

- Write a book review on your blog or on a retailer site.

- Pick up a copy for friends, family, or anyone who you think
  would enjoy and be challenged by its message!

- Share this message on social media:
  I loved #breakthefear by @Maria.Furlough // @RevellBooks

- Recommend this book for your church, workplace,
  book club, or small group.

- Follow Revell on social media and tell us what you like.